The Doctrine of the Real Presence As Set Forth in the Works of Divines and Others of the English Church Since the Reformation [Ed. by E.B. Pusey]. - Primary Source Edition

Edward Bouverie Pusey

Nabu Public Domain Reprints:

You are holding a reproduction of an original work published before 1923 that is in the public domain in the United States of America, and possibly other countries. You may freely copy and distribute this work as no entity (individual or corporate) has a copyright on the body of the work. This book may contain prior copyright references, and library stamps (as most of these works were scanned from library copies). These have been scanned and retained as part of the historical artifact.

This book may have occasional imperfections such as missing or blurred pages, poor pictures, errant marks, etc. that were either part of the original artifact, or were introduced by the scanning process. We believe this work is culturally important, and despite the imperfections, have elected to bring it back into print as part of our continuing commitment to the preservation of printed works worldwide. We appreciate your understanding of the imperfections in the preservation process, and hope you enjoy this valuable book.

THE DOCTRINE

OF

THE REAL PRESENCE

AS

SET FORTH IN THE WORKS

OF

DIVINES AND OTHERS

OF

THE ENGLISH CHURCH

SINCE

THE REFORMATION.

Dread of Transubstantiation has made the Sacrament a ceremony.
   KNOX'S *Remains*, Vol. i. p. 48.

Part I.

OXFORD AND LONDON:
JOHN HENRY PARKER, 377, STRAND.
1855.

LONDON:
G. J. PALMER, SAVOY STREET, STRAND.

ADVERTISEMENT.

THE following Catena has been drawn up at the request of a few friends who desired to have a succinct statement of the opinions of the principal divines and other members of the Church of England, who, since the Reformation, have vindicated the doctrine of a REAL PRESENCE in the Holy Sacrament. The Editor, having had but a very limited time for the work, has been obliged to publish it in a less complete form than he could have desired. He trusts, in a Second Part, to make it more perfect, and to add extracts from the works of some of the leading foreign Protestant writers. The present extracts are taken exclusively from authors who have entertained what is termed " high Eucharistic doctrine;" or, in other words, who have held a real and supernatural Presence of the Body and Blood of Christ, given either *in* or *by* the Consecrated Elements. The Editor has avoided giving any passages from the writings of such as have held what are called " low views" concerning this Holy Sacrament, whether these views are limited to " a quickened apprehension," according to the sentiments of Zuinglius and his followers, to a simple "act of Church-membership," as maintained by some modern writers, or to the merely figurative presence, of the followers of Hoadley, who reduce the Sacrament to a bare commemorative rite, or, as it has been, with sad irreverence, expressed, "the taking a glass of wine to the memory of the Founder of their faith."*

The Editor has added some explanatory Notes. These are all enclosed in brackets.

London, January 11, 1855.

* See "A Vindication of the Bishop of Winchester," London, 1736.

CONTENTS.

	PAGE
Act of Uniformity 2 & 3 Edward VI. ch. 1 (1549)	1
Act of Uniformity 5 & 6 Edward VI. (1552)	2
First Prayer Book of Edward VI.	3
Ridley	7
Cranmer	19
Poynet	21
Sutton	30
Hooker	32
Jackson	44
Donne	46
Andrewes	48
Royal Declaration	51
Articles relating to the Sacraments	52
The Golden Canons	61
Prayer Book of the Church of Ireland	63
The Protestation or Black Rubric	63
Overall	65

	PAGE
Church Catechism	71
The Homilies	73
Herbert	80
Taylor	81
Cosin	97
Thorndike	100
L'Estrange	119
Bull	120
Morton	121
Montague	121
Mede	121
Bramhall	124
Field	126
Forbes	126
Sparrow	127
Ken	128
Sherlock	129
Lake	130
Tillotson	131
Wheatly	131
Pelling	133
Burnet	145
Nelson	150
Wilson	152
Grabe	153
Randolph	154

						PAGE
Warburton	.	.	.	.	.	154
Palmer .	.	.	.	.	.	156
Harold Brown	.	.	.	.	.	165
Beaumont	.	.	.	.	.	169

ERRATA.

Page 8, line 3, *for* " Norton " *read* " Weston."
,, 8, line 8, *add* " Ibid. p. 251."
,, 9, line 1 and 2, *for* " by mystery and grace," *read* " in mystery and by grace."
,, 9, line 3, *for* " here " *read* " Him."
,, 9, line 5, *for* " charity," *read* " drinking."
,, 10, line 7, *for* " the " *read* " His."
,, 11, line 19, *for* " to do " *read* " so to do."
,, 13, line 24, *for* " It is instituted of God ?" *read* " It is instituted of God."
,, 13, line 25, *for* " In the Supper?" *read* " In the Supper."
,, 16, line 11, *dele* " said."
,, 17, before the note * supply [.
,, 17, line 17, *for* " bear " *read* " bare."
,, 17, line 35, *for* " 206 " *read* " 205."
,, 18, line 17, *add* " Ibid. pp. 236—245."
,, 51, line 23, *for* " 26, 7," *read* " 266, 7."
,, 51, line 25, *for* " substantice " *read* " substantiæ."
,, 79, note, line 10, *for* " dixit " *read* " dicit."
,, 79, ,, line 12, *for* " palmorum," *read* " palmarum."
,, 101, line 29, *for* " though " *read* " through."
,, 103, line 6, *for* " are " read " in."
,, 107, line 24, *dele* " ª."
,, 108, line 4 from bottom, *for* " ª " *read* " it."
,, 109, line 3, *for* " ; rather " *read* " ? Rather"
,, 112, line 7, after " Flesh and Blood " *read* " of that incarnate Jesus; where, by comparing the Eucharist with the Flesh and Blood."
,, 112, line 7, *for* " followed him. He " *read* " followed him, he."
,, 112, line 25, after " again " *for* " ? " *read* " ."

EXTRACTS

FROM

THE WRITINGS OF DIVINES AND OTHERS

OF THE

ENGLISH CHURCH,

SINCE

THE PERIOD OF THE REFORMATION,

WHO

HAVE DENIED BOTH THE PHYSICAL* AND
THE MERELY FIGURATIVE, AND HELD THE REAL AND
ESSENTIAL PRESENCE OF THE BODY AND BLOOD
OF CHRIST IN THE HOLY EUCHARIST.

From the Act of Uniformity, 2 & 3 Edward VI. c. 1.

"His Highness .... hath appointed the Archbishop of Canterbury, and certain of the most learned and discreet Bishops, and other learned men of this realm, to consider and ponder the premises, and thereupon having as well eye and respect to the most sincere and pure Christian religion taught by the Scripture, as to the usages in the primitive Church, should draw and make one convenient and meet order rite and fashion of common and open Prayer and administration of the Sacraments, to be had and used in his Majesty's Realm of England and

[The Book of Common Prayer unanimously adopted by the Archbishop, Bishops, and other learned men, and concluded by the aid of the Holy Ghost.]

[* The Statute, 31° Henry VIII. c. 14 (that of the Six Articles), enforces a belief of "Transubstantiation, or the entire physical change of the elements in the Eucharist."]

<small>Act of uniformity.</small> in Wales: the which at this time, by the aid of the Holy Ghost, with one uniform agreement is of them concluded, set forth, and delivered to his Highness, <small>Received by the King to his comfort.</small> to his great comfort and quietness of mind, in a book entitled The Book of Common Prayer, and administration of the Sacraments, and other rites and ceremonies of the Church after the use of the Church of England." . . . .

From the Act of Uniformity, 5 & 6 Edward (1552).

"Where there hath been a very godly order set forth by authority of Parliament, for common Prayer and administration of the Sacraments, to be used in <small>The same book approved of.</small> the mother tongue, within this Church of England, agreeable to the Word of God and the Primitive Church, very comfortable to all good people. . . .

"And because there hath arisen in the use and exercise of the aforesaid Common Service of the Church heretofore set forth, divers doubts for the <small>But altered by reason of the curiosity of the minister and mistakers.</small> fashion and manner of the ministration of the same, rather by the curiosity of the minister and mistakers, than of any other worthy cause . . . . The King's Most Excellent Majesty, with the assent of the Lords and Commons in the present Parliament assembled, and by the authority of the same, hath caused the foresaid order of Common Service, entitled *The Book of Common Prayer*, to be faithfully <small>Explained and perfected.</small> and godly perused, explained, and made fully perfect, and by the foresaid authority hath annexed and joined it, so explained and perfected, to this present statute, &c.*

[* The Rev. Thomas Bowyer, M.A., Vicar of Martock in Somersetshire, in his "Treatise on the Sacrament," London,

FIRST PRAYER BOOK OF KING EDWARD VI., *approved by Convocation*, 1549. (See Strype.)

From the Prayer of Access.

" Grant us, therefore, gracious Lord, so to eat the flesh of thy dear Son Jesus Christ, and to drink His

1736, in reply to Hoadley's " Plain Account," makes the following observations in regard to the authority of this Act :—

" I observe, 2ndly. That from the sacrificial expressions of the first Liturgy of Edward VI. (in which the oblation and invocation were expressly retained), it is evident that our first Reformers believed the Lord's Supper to be a *Sacrifice*.

" 3rdly. That though in the second Liturgy of Edward VI. some expressions were left out, yet the Church did not then alter her opinion with respect to the doctrine of the Sacrifice; because, at the same time, in the same Act of Parliament, which enacted the alterations, it was declared that the *first* Book for Administration of the Sacraments was agreeable to the Word of God and the primitive Church; and that the *alterations were made rather by the curiosity of the minister (perhaps Bucer is meant) and mistakers, than of any other worthy cause.*

" This Act of Parliament was repealed by Queen Mary, revived by Queen Elizabeth, and confirmed by King Charles II. after the Restoration, at which time the Rubric relating to the time when, and the person by whom (the Priest, whilst the sentences are read), together with the word Oblations in the Prayer for the whole estate &c., were added, probably by Heylin, Bishop Thorndyke, and others, who thought the Sacrament a sacrifice : and it was to be wished that this Rubric were unscrupulously observed. So that this Act is still in force, and though some expressions are left out, and some alterations made, yet the doctrine of our Church, with respect to the sacrifice of the Sacrament, altereth not." This argument, of course, applies equally to all other doctrines contained in Edward's first Book. Even Cranmer thought it not unlawful to use the offices in this Book, after the introduction of the second Book, in which he had so large a share, having celebrated the Eucharist according to the form contained therein at the funeral of King Edward.]

blood, in these holy mysteries, that we may continually dwell in Him and He in us, that our sinful bodies may be made clean by His body, and our souls washed through his most precious blood."

From the Exhortations to Communion.

"Therefore if any here be a blasphemer, &c., let him bewail his sins, and not come to that holy table; lest after the taking of that most blessed bread, the devil enter into him as he did into Judas," &c.

" . . . He hath left us in those holy mysteries as a pledge of his love, and a continual remembrance of the same, his own blessed Body and precious Blood, for us to feed upon spiritually, to our endless comfort and consolation."

"Wherefore our duty is to come to these holy mysteries with most heavenly thanks to be given to Almighty God, for his infinite mercy and benefits given and bestowed upon us His unworthy servants, for whom He hath not only given His Body to death, and shed His Blood, but also doth vouchsafe in a sacrament* and mystery, to give us His said Body and Blood to feed upon spiritually."

[* The above sentence was thus altered in Edward VIth's second Prayer Book, so as to exclude, or at least neutralize, the idea of Christ's presence in the Sacrament: "Our duty is to render to Almighty God our heavenly Father most hearty thanks, for that He hath given his Son, our Saviour Jesus Christ, not only to die for us, but also to be our spiritual food and sustenance, *as it is declared unto us, as well by God's word as by the holy Sacraments of His Body and Blood.*" At the last revision, however, of the Book of Common Prayer, it was restored as it now stands: "It is our duty to render most humble and hearty thanks to Almighty God our heavenly Father,

"As the benefit is great, if with a truly penitent heart and lively faith we receive that Holy Sacrament, for then we *spiritually* eat the Flesh of Christ and drink His Blood, then we dwell in Christ and Christ in us. We be made one with Christ, and Christ, with us. So is the danger great if we receive the same unworthily, for then we become guilty of the Body and Blood of Christ our Saviour. We eat and drink our own damnation, not considering the Lord's Body."* Edward VI. First Book.

From the Consecration Prayer (which had then no title).†

"With Thy Holy Spirit and Word vouchsafe to bless and sanctify these Thy gifts and creatures of bread and wine, that they may be unto us the Body and Blood of Thy most dearly beloved Son Jesus Christ, who in the same night, &c. For the descent of the Holy Spirit.

"Humbly beseeching Thee that whosoever shall be partakers of this Holy Communion [may worthily for that He hath given his Son our Saviour Jesus Christ, not only to die for us, but also to be our spiritual food and sustenance n that holy Sacrament."]

[* This exhortation first appeared in the Order of Communion in 1548, before any change was introduced into the doctrine of the real Presence, as contained in "the King's Book," and has been included, with a few verbal alterations, in every successive revision of the Book of Common Prayer. In this Book (*The Necessary Doctrine of a Christian Man*), which contained the law of the Church as binding during the whole of Edward's reign, the DOCTRINE is thus stated: "In this worshipful Sacrament of the altar the creatures which be taken to the use thereof, as bread and wine, do not remain still in their own substance, but by the virtue of Christ's word in the consecration, be changed and turned into the very substance of the Body and Blood of our Saviour Jesus Christ."]

[† See Part II., Appendix.]

Edward VI. First Book.

receive the most precious Body and Blood of Thy Son Jesus Christ, and be fulfilled] * with Thy grace and heavenly benediction, and made one body with Thy Son Jesus Christ, that He may dwell in them and they in Him."

From the Post Communion.

"We most heartily thank Thee, for that Thou hast vouchsafed to feed us in these holy mysteries, with the spiritual food of the most precious Body and Blood of Thy Son our Saviour Jesus Christ, and hast assured us (duly receiving the same) of Thy power and goodness towards us."

From the Rubric at the end of the Communion Service.

"For avoiding all matters and occasion of dissension, it is meet that the bread prepared for the Communion be made, through all this realm, after one sort and fashion: that is to say, unleavened and round, as it was afore, but without all manner of print, and something more larger and thicker than it was, so that it may be aptly divided in divers pieces; and every one shall be divided in two pieces at the least, or more, by the discretion of the minister, and so distributed. And men must not think less to be received in part than in the whole, but in each of them the whole body of our Saviour Jesus Christ."†

The whole body of Christ received by each.

[* The bracketted passage was omitted in Edward's Second Book, but restored in the Scotch Communion Book in 1636, and is still used in the Communion Service of the Church in Scotland. It was also restored in the American Book of Common Prayer, in 1789.]

[† This rubric was omitted at the desire of Bucer, on the principle that "it might give occasion to the ignorant or contentious to suppose that the Body and Blood of Christ was

RIDLEY.

[Chaplain to Archbishop Cranmer, 1537; Master of Pembroke, Chaplain to Henry VIII., and D.D., 1540; Bishop of Rochester, 1547; Bishop of London, 1550; suffered martyrdom under Queen Mary, October 16th, 1555.]

From his Disputation at Oxford, April, 1555.

" Evil men do eat the very true and natural Body of Christ sacramentally, and no further, as S. Augustine saith ; but good men do eat the very true Body, both sacramentally, and spiritually by grace."—*Remains*, p. 246.

<small>The natural Body eaten by the wicked, but only sacramentally; by good men spiritually.</small>

Again,—

" We worship, I confess, the same true Lord and Saviour of the world, which the wise men worshipped in the manger ; howbeit, we do it in a mystery, and in the Sacrament of the Lord's Supper, and that in spiritual liberty, not in carnal servitude ; that is, we do not worship servilely the signs for the things ; . . . . . but we behold with the eyes of faith Him present after grace, and spiritually set upon the table ; and we worship Him which sitteth above, and is

<small>Augustin de Doct. Christ.</small>

<small>The things, not the signs, objects of worship in the Lord's Supper.</small>

offered as if locally included in the particles of bread." He, therefore, recommends that it be omitted, or replaced by an explanation—" that this breaking of the bread and distribution of the particles, is only directed in order more fully to represent what our Lord did in His last supper—and that He meant to impart the food of everlasting life to each communicant at His Table. For that it was of itself known to the faithful, that the fraction and partition of the symbol did not in any wise detract from the true and solid reception and communication of the Body of Christ, which is effected by the Spirit." (Id enim fidelibus per se notum esse perceptioni et communicationi veræ et solidæ corporis Christi, quæ scilicet fit Spiritu, symboli fractionem et partitionem omnino nihil detrahere).—Buceri Censura.]

<small>Ridley.</small>

worshipped of the angels. For Christ is always assistant to his mysteries, as S. Augustine saith," &c.

" *Norton.*—That which the woman did hold in her womb; the same thing holdeth the priest.

<small>Christ held in his hands his natural Body, but the priest the mystery of the Body.</small>

" *Ridley.*—I grant the priest holdeth the same thing, but after another manner. He did hold the natural Body, the priest doth hold the mystery of the Body."*

[In reply to Dr. Smith, who had cited Chrysostom as saying, "O miracle, O good will of God! He that sitteth above, at the sacrifice time is contained in the hands of men."†]

[* "Here Ridley draws the correct distinction between the subjective and the objective presence of Christ in the Sacrament. To all He is outwardly and sacramentally present in the consecrated elements, but to the faithful and penitent only is He present inwardly and spiritually. All eat the flesh of Christ orally, but those only eat *spiritually* as well as sacramentally, who come with a true penitent heart and lively faith. 'Then,' to use the language of our Church, and then only, do 'we *spiritually* eat the flesh of Christ, and drink His blood.' The wicked and those that be devoid of a lively faith eat not, as S. Augustine says, the Body and Blood of Christ; that is, as he explains it, they eat it temporally and outwardly only, not inwardly and spiritually. We should have avoided many errors in our mode of speaking on this subject, if we, like Ridley, made the logical distinction between the inward and subjective and outward and objective presence of Christ in the Sacrament.

"It is evident from these passages that the word *spiritually* refers to the disposition of the communicant, and that it is thereby beyond question implied in the Liturgy of the Church of England, that there is a real objective presence, irrespective of the faith of the communicant."—*Ecclesiastic*, November, 1854.]

† ʼΩ τοῦ θαύματος· ʼΩ τῆς τοῦ Θεοῦ φιλανθρωπίας· ὁ μετὰ τοῦ πατρὸς ἄνω καθήμενος κατὰ τὴν ὥραν ἐκείνην ταῖς ἁπάντων κατέχεται χερσὶ καὶ δίδωσιν αὑτὸν τοῖς βουλομένοις περιπτύξασθαι καὶ περιλαβεῖν. S. Chrys. de Sacerdotio, lib. iii. cap. 4. Op. Ed. Ben. Par. 1718, tom. i. p. 382.

"He that sitteth there is *here* present by mystery and grace; and is holden of the godly, such as communicate here, not only sacramentally with the hand of the body, but, much more, wholesomely, with the hand of the heart, and by inward charity is received; but the sacramental signification is holden of all men."—P. 223.

<small>Ridley.</small>

"Furthermore the said Theophylact, writing upon these words, 'This is my body,' sheweth, that the body of the Lord is bread, which is sanctified on the altar.

"*Oglethorp*:—That place of Theophylact maketh openly against you: for he saith in that place, that Christ said not, 'This is the figure of my body, but my body.' 'For,' saith he, 'by an unspeakable operation it is transformed, although it seem to us to be bread.'

"*Ridley*:—It is not a figure; that is to say, 'Non tantum est figura;' i. e. It is not only a figure of his body.

"*Weston*:—Where have you that word 'tantum,' 'only'?

"*Ridley*:—It is not in that place, but he hath it in another; and Augustine doth so speak many times, and other doctors more."

"I grant the bread to be converted and turned into the Flesh of Christ; but not by transubstantiation, but by sacramental converting or turning. 'It is transformed,' saith Theophylact in the same place, 'by a mystical benediction, and by the accession or coming of the Holy Ghost unto the Flesh of Christ.

<small>In reply to Weston, who had cited Theophylact, to prove that it was no figure.</small>

Ridley. He saith not by expulsion or driving away the substance of bread, and by substituting or putting in its place the corporal substance of Christ's Flesh. And whereas he saith, 'It is not a figure of the body,' we should understand that saying, as he himself does elsewhere, add 'only,' that is, it is no naked or bare figure *only.* For Christ is present *in* the mysteries; neither at any time, as Cyprian saith, doth the Divine Majesty abstract Himself from the Divine mysteries. —*Ibid.* p. 230.

<small>Ceres and Bacchus said to be worshipped by the Christians.</small>

"*Glyn.*—Augustine against Faustus [saith,] 'Some there were which thought us, instead of the bread and of the cup, to worship Ceres and Bacchus.' Upon this place I gather, that there was an adoration of the Sacrament among the Fathers; and Erasmus, in an epistle to the brethren of Low Germany, saith, that the worshipping of the sacrament was before Augustine and Cyprian.

"*Ridley.*—We do handle the signs reverently: but we worship the sacrament as a sacrament, not as the thing signified by the Sacrament.

"*Glyn.*—What is the symbol or sacrament?

"*Ridley.*—Bread.

"*Glyn.*—Ergo, we worship bread.

"*Ridley,*—There is a deceit in this word 'adoramus.' We worship the symbols, when reverently we handle them. We worship Christ wheresoever we perceive his benefits; but we understand his benefits to be greatest in the Sacrament.

"*Glyn.*—So I may fall down before the bench here, and worship Christ; and if any man ask me what I do, I may answer, I worship Christ."

"*Ridley.*—We adore and worship Christ in the Eucharist. And if you mean the external Sacrament, I say, that also is to be worshipped as a Sacrament.

"*Glyn.*—So was the faith of the primitive Church.

"*Ridley.*—Would to God we would all follow the faith of that church!

"*Glyn.*—Think you that Christ hath now his Church?

"*Ridley.*—I do so.

"*Glyn.*—But all the church adoreth Christ verily and really in the sacrament.

"*Ridley.*—You know yourself that the Eastern Church would not acknowledge transubstantiation; as appeareth in the council of Florence.

"*Cole.*—That is false: for in the same they did acknowledge transubstantiation; although they would not entreat of that matter, for that they had not in their commission to do.

"*Ridley.*—Nay, they would determine nothing of the matter, when the article was propounded unto them.

"*Cole.*—It was not because they did not acknowledge the same, but because they had no commission so to do.

"*Curtop.*—Reverend sir, I will prove and declare, that the body of Christ is truly and really in the Eucharist: and whereas the holy Fathers, both of the East and West Church, have written both many things and no less manifest of the same matter, yet will I bring forth only Chrysostom. The place is this: *

"* Τοῦτο τὸ ἐν ποτηρίῳ ὂν, ἐκεῖνο ἐστὶ τὸ ἀπὸ τῆς πλευρας ῥεῦσαν·

<small>Ridley.</small>

"'That which is in the cup is the same that flowed from the side of Christ.

"'But true and pure blood did flow from the side of Christ:

"Ergo, His true and pure blood is in the cup.

"*Ridley.*—It is his true blood which is in the chalice, I grant, and the same which sprang from the side of Christ. But how? It is blood indeed, but not after the same manner, after which manner it sprang from his side. For here is his blood, but by way of a Sacrament. Again I say, like as the bread of the Sacrament and of thanksgiving is called the body of Christ given for us; so the cup of the Lord is called the blood which sprang from the side of Christ; but that sacramental bread is called the body, because it is the Sacrament of his body. Even so likewise the cup is called the blood also which flowed out of Christ's side, because it is the sacrament of that blood which flowed out of his side, instituted of the Lord himself for our singular commodity, namely, for our spiritual nourishment; like as baptism is ordained in water to our spiritual regeneration.

"*Curtop.*—The sacrament of the blood is not the blood.

"*Ridley.*—The sacrament of the blood is the blood; <small>Res sacramenti.</small> and that is attributed to the sacrament, which is spoken of the thing of the sacrament.

"*Weston.*—That is very well. Then we have blood in the chalice.

"*Ridley.*—It is true; but by grace, and in a sacrament.

καὶ ἐκείνου μετέχομεν. S. Chrys. in cap. x. Cor. 1. Hom. xxiv. Op. Ed. Ben. Par. 1732, tom. x. pp. 212—13.

"(Here the people hissed at him.)

"*Ridley.*—O my masters! I take this for no judgment: I will stand to God's judgment.

"*Watson.*—Good sir, I have determined to have respect to the time, and to abstain from all those things which may hinder the entrance of our disceptation: and therefore first I ask this question: When Christ said, in John vi., 'He that eateth my flesh,' &c., doth he signify in those words the eating of his true and natural flesh, or else of the bread and symbol?

"*Ridley.*—I understand that place of the very flesh of Christ to be eaten, but spiritually: and further I say, that the sacrament also pertaineth unto the spiritual manducation: for without the spirit to eat the sacrament, is to eat it unprofitably; for whoso eateth not spiritually, he eateth his own condemnation.

"*Watson.*—I ask then, whether the eucharist be a sacrament?

"*Ridley.*—The eucharist, taken for a sign or symbol, is a sacrament.

"*Watson.*—Is it instituted of God?

"*Ridley.*—It is instituted of God?

"*Watson.*—Where?

"*Ridley.*—In the Supper?

"*Watson.*—With what words is it made a sacrament?

"*Ridley.*—By the words and deeds which Christ said and did, and commanded us to say and do the same.

"*Watson.*—It is a thing commonly received of all, that the sacraments of the new law give grace to them that worthily receive.

Ridley.

"*Ridley.*—True it is, that grace is given by the sacrament; but as by an instrument. The inward virtue and Christ give the grace through the sacrament.

* * * * *

"*Ridley.*—There is no promise made to them that receive common bread, as it were; but to those that worthily receive the sanctified bread there is a promise of grace made, like as Origen doth testify.

"*Watson.*—Where is that promise made?

"*Ridley.*—'The bread which we break, is it not a communication of the body of Christ?' And 'we being many are one bread, one body of Christ.'

"*Watson.*—What doth he mean by bread in this place?

"*Ridley.*—The bread of the Lord's table, the communion of the body of Christ.

"*Watson.*—Hearken what Chrysostom saith upon that place: * 'The bread which we break, is it not the communication of Christ's body?' Wherefore did he not say participation? Because he would signify some greater matter, and that he would declare a great convenience and conjunction betwixt the same. For we do not communicate by participation only and receiving, but also by co-uniting; for likewise as that body is co-united to Christ, so

---

* Ὁ ἄρτος ὃν κλῶμεν, οὐχὶ κοινωνία τοῦ σώματος τοῦ Χρίστου ἐστί; διὰ τί μὴ εἶπε μετοχή; ὅτι πλέον τι δηλῶσια ἠβουλήθη, καὶ πολλὴν ἐνδείξασθαι τὴν συνάφειαν· οὐ γὰρ τῷ μετέχειν μόνον καὶ μεταλαμβάνειν, ἀλλὰ καὶ τῷ ἑνοῦσθαι κοινωνοῦμεν. καθάπερ γὰρ τὸ σῶμα ἐκεῖνο ἥνωται τῷ Χριστῷ, οὕτω δὲ ἡμεῖς αὐτῷ διὰ τοῦ ἄρτου τούτου ἑνούμεθα.—S. Chrysost. Hom. xxiv. in 1 Corinth. cap. x. Op. Ed. Ben. Par. 1718, tom. x. p. 213.

also we, by the same bread, are conjoined and united to him.

"*Ridley.*—Let Chrysostom have his manner of speaking and his sentence. If it be true, I reject it not. But let it not be prejudicial to me, to name it true bread.

"*Watson.*—'All,' saith Chrysostom, 'which sit together at one board, do communicate together of one true body. What do I call,' saith he, 'this communicating? We are all the selfsame body. What doth bread signify? The body of Christ. What be they that receive it? The body of Christ: for many are but one body.' Chrysostom doth interpret this place against you: 'All we be one bread and one mystical body, which do participate together one bread of Christ.'*

"*Ridley.*—All we be one mystical body, which do communicate of one Christ in bread, after the efficacy of regeneration or quickening.

"*Watson.*—Of what manner of bread speaketh he?

"*Ridley.*—Of the bread of the Lord's table.

* * * * *

"*Smith.*—I bring here Augustine expounding these words, 'He was carried in his own hands:'†

---

* Τὶ γὰρ λέγω κοινωνίαν, φησίν: αὐτό ἐσμεν ἐκεῖνο τὸ σῶμα· τί γὰρ ἐστὶν ὁ ἄρτος; σῶμα Χριστοῦ. τί δὲ γίνονται οἱ μεταλαμβάνοντες; σῶμα Χριστοῦ, οὐχὶ σώματα πολλὰ ἀλλὰ σῶμα ἕν. S. Chrysost. Hom. xxiv. in 1 Corinth. cap. x. Op. Ed. Ben. Par. 1718, tom. x. p. 213.

† Hoc vero, fratres, quomodo possit fieri in homine, quis intelligat? Manibus enim suis nemo portatur, sed alienis. Quomodo intelligatur de David secumdum literam, non invenimus; de

Ridley. How may this be understood to be done in man? For no man is carried in his own hands, but in the hands of other. How this may be understood of David after the letter, we do not find; of Christ we find it. For Christ was borne in his own hands, when he saith, 'This is my body:' for he carried that same body in his own hands, &c. Augustine here did not see how this place, after the letter, could be understood of David; because no man can carry himself in his own hands. 'Therefore,' saith he, 'this place is said to be understood of Christ after the letter.' For Christ carried himself in his own hands in his Supper, when he gave the sacrament to his disciples, saying, 'This is my body.'

"*Ridley.*—I deny your argument, and I explicate the same. Augustine could not find, after his own understanding, how this could be understood of David after the letter. Augustine goeth here from others in this exposition, but I go not from him. But let this exposition of Augustine be granted to you; although I know this place of Scripture be otherwise read of other men, after the verity of the Hebrew text, and it is also otherwise to be expounded. Yet, to grant to you this exposition of Augustine, I say yet notwithstanding, it maketh nothing against my assertion: for Christ did bear himself in his own hands, when he gave the sacrament of his body to be eaten of his disciples.

Christo autem invenimus. Ferebatur enim Christus in manibus suis cum diceret, Hoc est corpus meum. Ferebat enim illud corpus in manibus suis, quando commendans ipsum corpus suum diceret Hoc est corpus meum, etc.—S. Aug. in Psal. xxxiii. Enar. Op. Ed. Ben. Par. 1685, tom. iv. col. 214.

"*Smith.*—Ergo, It is true of Christ after the letter, that he was borne in his own hands.

"*Ridley.*—He was borne literally, and after that letter which was spoken of David: but not after the letter of these words, 'Hoc est corpus meum.'

"I grant that St. Augustine saith, that it is not found literally of David, that he carried himself in his own hands, and that it is found of Christ. But this word 'ad literam,' 'literally,' you do not well refer to that which was borne, but rather it ought to be referred to him that did bear it. St. Augustine's meaning is this; that it is not read anywhere in the Bible, that this carnal David, the Son of Jesse, did bear himself in his hands; but of that spiritual David, that overthrew Goliath the devil (that is, of Christ our Saviour, the son of the Virgin), it may well be found literally, that he bear himself in his own hands after a certain manner, namely, in carrying the sacrament of himself. And note, that St. Augustine hath these words, 'quodam modo,' 'after a certain manner;' which manifestly declare, how the doctor's meaning is to be taken.*

* "Et ferebatur in manibus suis: Quomodo ferebatur in manibus suis? Quia cum commendaret ipsum corpus suum et sanguinem suum, accepit in manus suas quod norunt fideles, et ipse portabat quodam modo, cum diceret 'Hoc est,'" &c. In Ps. xxxiii. Enar. 2.

In reference to this subject Jahn (Enchiridion Hermeueuticæ, Vienna, 1804, § 11, p. 36) observes: "Qui ergo, *e. g.* dicit Apostolos in ultima cœna non potuisse verba, a Jesu prolata, de sumtione corporis et sanguinis Ipsius, quem adcumbentem secum cernebant, intelligere, nihil proficit; præsertim cum Paulus, 1 Cor. xi. 27, hac de re sublimius doceat."

The following passage from another of Augustine's works referred to by Ridley in the same disputation (*Remains*, p. 206.),

Ridley.

"*Smith.*—When then was he borne in his own hands, and after what letter?

"*Ridley.*—He was borne in the supper sacramentally, when he said, 'This is my body.'

"*Smith.*—Every man may bear in his own hands a figure of his body. But Augustine denieth that David could carry himself in his hands :

"Ergo, He speaketh of no figure of his body.

"*Ridley.*—If Augustine could have found in all the Scripture, that David had carried the sacrament of his body, then he would never have used that exposition of Christ.

"*Smith.*—But he did bear himself in his own hands :

"Ergo, He did not bear a figure only.

"*Ridley.*—He did bear himself, but in a sacrament: and Augustine afterwards addeth, 'quodam modo,' that is, 'sacramentally.'

Bertram counted a Catholic for 700 years.

"I have also for proof of what I have spoken, whatsoever Bertram, a man learned, of sound and upright judgment, and ever counted a catholic for these seven hundred years, until this our age, hath

further illustrates that Father's meaning, and serve to show that while maintaining a true Sacramental Presence, he did not believe in a physical one: "Nonne semel immolatus est Christus in seipso, et tamen in sacramento non solum per omnes paschæ solemnitates, sed omni die populis immolatur: nec utique mentitus, qui interrogatus, eum responderit immolari. Si enim sacramenta quandam similitudinem earum rerum, quarum sacramenta sunt, non haberent, omnino sacramenta non essent. Ex hac autem similitudine plerumque etiam ipsarum rerum nomina accipiunt. Sicut ergo secundum quendam modum, sacramentum corporis Christi, corpus Christi est, sacramentum sanguinis Christi, sanguis Christi est, ita sacramentum fidei, fides est."—*Aug. Epist. Bonif.* ep. xxiii. Opera, ii. 28.]

written. His treatise, whoever shall read, or weigh, considering the time of the writer, his learning, godliness of life, the allegations of the ancient Fathers, and his manifold and most grounded arguments, I cannot doubtless, but much marvel, if he have any fear of God at all, how he can with good conscience, speak against him, in this matter of the Sacrament. This Bertram was the first that pulled me by the ear, and that first brought me from the common error of the Romish Church, and caused me to search more diligently and exactly both the Scriptures and the writings of the old ecclesiastical Fathers in this matter."—*Works*, p. 206. (*Parker Society's edition.*)

CRANMER.

[Thomas Cranmer, born 1489; Archbishop of Canterbury, 1533; suffered death for his religion, 1555.]

"I say that the same visible and palpable flesh that was for us crucified, ... is eaten of Christian people at His Holy Supper .... The diversity is not in the Body, but in the eating thereof; no man eating it carnally, but the good eating it both sacramentally and spiritually, and the evil only sacramentally" ..... —*Remains*, iii. 310; iii. 44; iv. 16.

"And touching my doctrine of the Sacrament (p. 195), and other my doctrine, of what kind soever it be, I protest that it was never my mind to write, speak, or understand, anything contrary to the most Holy Word of God, or else against the holy Catholic Church of Christ, but purely and simply to imitate

<small>Cranmer.</small> and teach those things only which I had learned out of the sacred Scriptures, and of the holy Catholic Church of Christ from the beginning, and also according to the exposition of the most holy and learned Fathers and Martyrs of the Church.

<small>Is ready to follow the judgment of the Church.</small> "And if anything hath peradventure chanced otherwise than I thought, I may err, but heretic I cannot be, forasmuch as I am ready in all things to follow the judgment of the most sacred Word of God, and of the holy Catholic Church, desiring none other mercy than meekly and gently to be taught, if anywhere (which God forbid) I have swerved from the truth.

"And I protest and openly confess that in all my doctrine and preaching, both of the Sacraments and of other my doctrine, whatsoever it be, not only I mean and judge those things as the Catholic Church and the most holy Fathers of old, with one accord, have meant and judged, but also I would gladly use the same words that they used, and not use any other words; but to set my hand to all and singular their speeches, phrases, ways, and forms of speech, which they do use in their treatise on the Sacrament, and <small>From his appeal at his degradation shortly before his death.</small> to keep and use their interpretation. But in this thing only I am accused for a heretic, because I allow not the doctrine lately brought in of the Sacrament, and because I consent not to words not accustomed in Scripture, and unknown to the ancient Fathers, but merely invented and brought in by men, and belonging to the destruction of souls and overthrowing of the old and pure religion."—*Works*, vol. iv. pp. 126, 127.

POYNET.

[John Poynet, born 1516; Bishop of Rochester, 1546; Winchester, 1551, 3 Edward VI. An eminent scholar and divine, and the most distinguished mathematician in Cambridge. On Mary's accession was expelled from his bishopric, and retired to Strasburg; died there in 1556, æt. 40.]

From his Treatise on the Eucharist, written during his exile, entitled "Diallacticon viri boni et literati, de veritate, natura, atque substantia Corporis et Sanguinis Christi in Eucharistia." 1st. ed., 1557; 2nd. ed., 1576; 3rd. ed., 1688; English Translation by Lady Russell, 1608. The following translation is by the Editor.

" The Body of Christ is at once truth and figure: truth, inasmuch as the Body and Blood of Christ is in its own virtue made from the substance of the Bread and Wine, but that which outwardly meets the senses is a figure." He thus concludes his treatise, (for an analysis of which see *infra*, "Johnson"):

" Here a scruple arises. If we believe the grace and virtue of the real body to be conjoined with the bread and wine, we shall seem to attribute too much to the elements, and hence a twofold evil will arise—(1) the adoration of the Sacrament and the peril of idolatry, and (2) that the wicked who partake of the Sacrament eat at the same time the Body of Christ, and are partakers of His grace. But this latter cannot take place, for 'Whoso eateth me,' saith Christ, 'shall live for ever,' and if any man eat of this bread he shall live for ever,' which cannot be understood of the wicked. As to the worship, I reply, that the ancients partook of the Sacrament with the utmost reverence and honour, and yet were safe from idolatry. . . . For as to their worshipping what they received, Augustine plainly

<small>Poynet.</small>

testifies on the xcviiith Psalm, when he says, 'He has given the same flesh to you to eat to salvation, but no one eats that flesh without first adoring, and not only do we not sin by adoring, but we sin by not adoring.' Also, Prosper, 'In the species of bread and wine which we see, we honour invisible things, that is, the Flesh and Blood.' Also, Eusebius Emissenus, 'When thou ascendest the reverend altar to be filled with spiritual food, behold, honour, and wonder at the holy body of thy God.' And Chrysostom, (1 Cor. x. Hom. xxiv.), 'I will show you upon earth what is worthy of this highest honour. For, as in palaces, not the walls, not the golden roof, but the royal body seated on the throne, is the most excellent of all; so also is the Royal Body in heaven now proposed to your view on earth. I do not show you angels nor archangels, nor the heaven of heavens, but the Lord of all these.' Ambrose (1 Cor. xi.), 'The Eucharist is spiritual medicine, which, tasted with reverence, purifies the devout receiver.' And again, 'The Holy Communion is to be approached with a devout mind, and with fear, that the mind may know that reverence is due to Him whose body it approaches to receive.' Theodoret (Dial. 2), 'Nor after sanctification do those mystical symbols differ from their proper nature, but remain in their former substance, and figure, and appearance (species) and are therefore both seen and felt as before. But they are understood to be that which they are made, and are believed to be so, and are worshipped, as being the things which they are believed.' From this and other places it is easily understood with what honour, with what reverence, the ancients approached to the Holy Commu-

<small>In Sententiis.</small>

nion. Nor is this to be wondered at, when they believed that they took, in that bread, the truth, nature, and virtue, of the true body of Christ, and were far from idolatry, being diligently instructed and taught that they did not worship the outward sign, but the inward virtue, which Augustin shows by these words (De Doct. Christ., lib. iii. cap. 9). 'For he but subserves the sign who performs or venerates any significant thing, not knowing what it signifies; but he who performs or venerates a useful sign instituted by God, the power and signification of which he understands, does not venerate the transient thing which he sees, but rather that to which all such things are to be referred.' And again, afterwards, 'At this time, by the resurrection of our Lord Jesus Christ, a more manifest proof of our liberty has taken place, nor are we burdened with the heavy load of those signs which we now understand, but the Lord and apostolic discipline have handed down, in place of many, some few things, and easy to be performed, as the Sacrament of Baptism, and the celebration of the Body and Blood of the Lord, which each person when he receives, being well instructed, knows what they signify, and worships them, not with carnal servitude, but with spiritual liberty.' Thus we see with what doctrine the Christians were formerly instructed, before they came to the use of these Sacraments, and how when they used honour or worship both in baptism and the celebration of the Supper, it was done without peril or scandal. Peril, inasmuch as it is hereby evident, that they did not look to the perishing thing which they saw, but to its virtue and signification. Scandal, because formerly it was their

Poynet.

religious discipline not only not to take the Sacrament before infidels, or those ignorant of the mysteries, but not even to speak before them of such sacred things. . . . . For it is worth while to observe that the ancients, when speaking of the Sacraments, used various terms, such as honouring, venerating, adoring, by which they meant to signify some other honour or reverence suitable to sacred things, as well as that worship prescribed by God, when He says, "Thou shalt worship the Lord thy God, and Him only shalt thou serve.' So that a double worship is here defined, one, that which we pay to God, the other, that which we give to signs and divine mysteries, according to the saying, 'Worship his footstool,' which many understand of the ark of the covenant, others of the humanity of Christ; or, if they think the same worship to be meant in both places, we may say that the flesh of Christ is to be adored, although a creature, by reason of the divinity to which it is united. The ark of the covenant was to be worshipped on account of the presence of the Divine majesty, which God himself promised. In the same manner we may worship the Eucharist, on account of the ineffable and invisible grace of Christ, as St. Augustine says, joined to it; not worshipping that which is visible and transient, but that which is believed and understood. . . .

Now as to the denial that the wicked can eat the body of Christ, which would necessarily be the case if virtue and spiritual grace were united with the bread, we must make a distinction. For, if we regard the nature of the Sacrament, Divine virtue cannot be absent from the sign, in so far as it is a Sacrament, and serves for this use ; if we look to the morals and mind of the recipient, it is not to him life and grace, both of which it is by its own nature, because the evil of the wicked is not capable of so great goodness, nor suffers it to bear fruit in itself. Nay, rather, it is death and condemnation to them. For, as many kinds of meats are in their own nature wholesome, but, if they enter into diseased bodies, increase the evil, and often accelerate death, not by their own nature but by the fault of the receiver ; so it is with regard to the Sacrament, in which its own virtue is always present, until it discharges its office ; although, when taken by the unworthy, he is not capable of receiving such goodness, or of deriving any profit therefrom. Cyprian confirms this. 'Sacraments, he says, cannot exist without their own virtue, nor can the Divine majesty be ever absent from the mysteries.' But although the Sacraments are permitted to be taken or touched by the unworthy, they whose want of faith or unworthiness resists so great holiness, cannot be partakers of the Spirit. Therefore to some these gifts are the savour of life unto life, to others the savour of death unto death, because it is altogether just that those who despise the grace should be deprived of so great benefit, and that purity should not make an abode for itself in those who are unworthy of such grace.

"Augustin says, 'Remember, therefore, that the manners of the wicked do not hinder the Sacraments, so that they either cease to be Sacraments altogether, or are less holy, but they harden evil men so that they have them as a witness of condemnation, not as an aid to salvation.' Also, in his fifth book (*de Bap-*

^{Poynet.} *tismo*) against the Donatists, c. 8, he observes: 'As Judas,' [&c., see *infra*, p. 59], so the body and blood of the Lord were not the less received even by those to whom the Apostle said, 'He that eateth and drinketh unworthily, eateth and drinketh his own con-
^{Contra Cres. lib. l. c. 25.} demnation.' And 'Although the Lord says, Unless a man eateth my flesh and drinketh my blood, he hath no life in him, does not the apostle teach that even this is pernicious to those who use it badly? For, he says, Whosoever shall eat this bread and drink this cup of the Lord unworthily, shall be guilty of the body and blood of the Lord.' . . . .

"From these and many places it is evident that the Eucharist, as far as appertains to the nature of the Sacrament, is truly the Body and Blood of Christ, is a truly Divine and holy thing, even when it is taken by the unworthy, while, however, they are not partakers of its grace and holiness, but drink their own death and condemnation. Nor in them does such goodness dwell, nor does it enter in order to dwell, but to condemn; nor does the contact of the Lord's body more profit them than it did the Jews to have touched that holy Body of His, always endowed with its own grace. Wherefore the Sacraments continue, so long as they are Sacraments, to retain their own virtue, nor can they be separated therefrom. For they always consist of their own parts—an earthly and a heavenly, a visible and an invisible, an inward and an outward, whether the good take them or the bad, whether the worthy or the unworthy. Besides, that commutation of the signs, and the transition of the elements into the inward substance, which everywhere occurs in the ancient writers, cannot exist, if we separate the virtue from the sign, and we wish the one to be taken apart from the other. But this is to be understood, so long as the sign serves its use, and is adapted to the end for which it was destined by the word of God. . . . . . The dignity of the Sacraments, and the honour due to them, is not injured, but remains whole and entire, so long as we confess that the truth of the Body and its nature and substance is received by the faithful, together with the symbols, as the ancient Fathers testify. Afterwards, when it is received (as the same Fathers have diligently observed), with this distinction between the proper or assumed body of Christ, and His symbolical body, or the Sacrament of His body, we do not err against the analogy of faith, which is not at all destroyed, inasmuch as we assign to each body its own attributes. For we say that the proper and assumed body is in place, and is circumscribed by space, after the manner of a true body, as S. Augustine says, as the true reason of human nature requires, and as "Orthodoxos" boldly affirmed against Eutyches and other heretics,—that they who deny it and affirm the ubiquity of that body, both deny thereby the true nature of a body, and fall into their errors and heresies. Nothing prevents the truth of the symbolical body notwithstanding, because it is a divine and spiritual thing, from being as widely diffused as the celebration of the Sacrament, according to the sentiment of the same "Orthodoxos." Besides which no absurdities accompany this doctrine, as many do the gross transubstantiation, as well as the carnal conjunction with the bread. . . . This explanation is neither perplexed nor difficult, but

Poynet. plain, as far as is compatible with the nature of mysteries. It contradicts no words of scripture, nor testimonies of the Fathers. It is ancient, and founded on the constant tradition of antiquity. It is not a new-fangled idea, and the invention of our own brain, but is a recalling of the primitive opinion of the Orthodox, and therefore strongly calculated to promote a reconciliation. . . . .

"Some are offended at the name of a sign or figure given to the Eucharist, as if it were a bare sign or mere empty figure. But here is not only a sign but the thing itself—not a figure only, but the very truth. Not content with this they appeal to the Fathers. They require the nature of a body in the Sacrament. Here then, too, is a presence of nature taught, and a natural participation effected. They still urge and demand that the *substance* of a body be confessed. They see the substance also affirmed by us to be present, and our communion with Christ naturally, and that I may so speak, substantially predicated; but these words must be understood not in the sense of philosophers but of theologians. Nor should we dispute as to the word transubstantiation, although barbarous and unnecessary, if only it was interpreted to mean such a transubstantiation as the ancients acknowledged, a sacramental change, such as takes place in a man regenerated by baptism, who becomes a new man and a new creature; such as takes place when we are converted into the flesh of Christ,—which illustrations are used by the ancient Fathers. We do not so much avoid the words as their meaning; and that signification which the Fathers teach, and argue, we also require. And it is only σαρκοφάγια, the feeding on flesh, which, far from approving, they

Transubstantiation a barbarous word, but capable of a good explanation.

It is only the eating of the natural flesh which is condemned.

condemn as foolish and impious, which we reject as foreign from the Scriptures, foreign from the interpretation of the Fathers, and diametrically opposed to the true faith; and we judge that a spiritual sense in eating the flesh is required by the authority of Christ himself, and the consent of the most approved interpreters. It is wonderful that, as in other controversies, we are Aristotelians, and catch at subtle rather than necessary distinctions, in these disputes about the Sacraments we admit of no difference, we receive no homonymy; when both the nature of the subject requires it, and the authority of the ancients points it out as with the finger: when neither the holy Scriptures nor the holy Fathers speak of the divine mysteries after a physical method, but in a sublime and divine manner, as becomes men who are θεολογοι, and θεοπνευστοι, comparing spiritual things with spiritual. Again, should there be any who think that *too* much is here ascribed to the elements, it is not so, but only its due reverence is given to the external symbols on account of their sacred use, and the inward virtue which is added by the power of the divine words is that alone which the mind of the faithful regards, which sanctifies both the body and mind of the receiver. But if some require a miracle (for some of the Fathers call the Eucharist a great miracle), it is no less truly wonderful that the earthly creatures of bread and wine, which were formed to nourish the body, should have that power planted *in* them by virtue of the mystical benediction, and therefore that they possess such potent efficacy, as to nourish, purify, sanctify, and prepare for immortality, both soul and body, and

Poynet.

Poynet. make us members of Christ and one body with Him. Nay, this miracle has greater weight, greater dignity, greater utility, and more agreeable to the nature of mysteries, than a gross transubstantiation or an animal or human σαρκοφαγια can afford. Wherefore the seeds of contention and discord are now removed, nor does there remain any cause why the Churches of Christ, especially those which profess the study of the Gospel, though they be now rent asunder by bitter hatreds, should not with united minds and joint affections coalesce together."

SUTTON.

[Christopher Sutton, Prebendary of Westminster; born, 1555; died, 1629.]

"13. Is it not a hard saying, 'Unless ye eat the flesh of the Son of God,' &c.? It is a hard saying to them that are hard of believing. The disciples hearing that of their Lord and Master, 'Take eat, this is My Body,' they take, they eat, asking no question. 'Being confirmed in faith,' saith St. Chrysostom, 'they take and eat: unbelievers hearing the same of our Saviour, they depart, they eat not.' Peter answereth, 'Lord, Thou hast the words of life;' others go backward, leaving the Lord of life. The Capernaite, hearing, dreameth of eating naturally, *The godly eat spiritually as well as really.* grossly; the godly are assured of eating spiritually, and yet withal really."

"32. Albeit then, the manner be not of us over curiously inquired or searched after, yet the same presence of Christ is acknowledged, which Christ Himself would have to be acknowledged. We say with

St. Ambrose, that there is not taken from bread the substance thereof, but that there is adjoined the grace of Christ's Body after a manner ineffable." Sutton.

"35. Last of all concerning the controversy about the holy Eucharist, between two extremes whereof we have heard, let us embrace the mean; let us, with a sincere faith, apprehend the truth; apprehending, let us keep it; keeping, let us adore it with godly manners.

"36. And now to draw in, as it were, the sails of this admonition, godly reader, seeing that this divine institution was left by our gracious Redeemer, both for the inward peace of the soul, and outward of the Church, who can sufficiently lament to see the dissension that hath miserably divided the Christian world, and discord that hath risen about the same! Let us call to mind that God is not the God of dissension but the God of peace. Let us all forbear on both sides, needless and unprofitable disputes. Unless thou, Lord, hadst said it, 'This is My Body, this is My Blood,' who would have believed it? Unless Thou hadst said, O holy Christ, 'Take, eat, drink ye all of this,' who durst have touched it? Who would have approached to so heavenly a repast, hadst Thou not commanded it, *hoc facite*, do ye this; but Thou commanding, who would not joyfully come and communicate? Hoc facite.

"37. Let us then hold captive human reason, and prepare ourselves unto the fruit of this heavenly manna. Unnecessary disputes bring small profits, we may with greater benefit wonder than argue. Then are the works of God most truly conceived, when they are devoutly admired."—*Godly Medita-*

Sutton. *tions on the Most Holy Sacrament of the Lord's Supper.* P. 299—301.

"Consider the Divine Wisdom of the Son of God, who, respecting our weakness, hath conveyed unto us His Body and Blood after a divine and spiritual manner, under the form of Bread and Wine." P. 26.

HOOKER.

[Richard Hooker, born 1554; Master of the Temple, 1584; died 1600.]

"As long as the days of our warfare last .... the words of our Lord and Saviour Christ will remain forcible : 'Except ye eat the flesh of the Son of Man, and drink his blood, ye have no life in you.'[*]

".... We understand that the strength of our life begun in Christ, is Christ; that his Flesh is meat and his blood drink, not by surmised imagination, but truly, even so truly that through faith we perceive in the Body and Blood sacramentally presented the very taste of eternal life, the grace of the Sacrament is here as the food which we eat and drink."

"This was it that some did exceedingly fear, lest Zuinglius and Œcolampadius would bring to pass, that men should account of this Sacrament but only as of a shadow, destitute, empty, and void of Christ. But seeing that by opening the several opinions which have been held, they are grown, for aught I can see, on all sides at the length, to a general agreement

[*] John vi. 53.

concerning that which alone is material, namely the *real participation* of Christ, and of life in his Body and Blood by means of this Sacrament, wherefore should the world continue still distracted and rent with so manifold contentions, when there remaineth now no controversy saving only upon the subject *where* Christ is? yea, even in this point, no side denieth but that the soul of man is the receptacle of Christ's presence, whereby the question is yet driven to a narrower issue; nor does anything rest doubtful but this, whether when the Sacrament is administered, Christ be wholly *within man only*, or else his Body and Blood be also externally seated in the very consecrated elements themselves;* which opinion they that defend are driven either to *consubstantiate* and incorporate Christ with elements sacramental, or to *transubstantiate* and change their substance into His; so the one to hold him really but invisibly moulded up with the substance of these elements, the other to hide him under the only visible show of bread and wine, the substance whereof, as they imagine, is abolished, and His succeeded in the same room."—(Book V. chap. lxvii. 2.)

"Sith we all agree that by the Sacrament Christ doth really and truly in us perform his promises, why do we vainly trouble ourselves with so fierce contentions, whether by consubstantiation or else by transubstantiation the Sacrament itself be first possessed with Christ or no? A thing which no way can further or hinder us, howsoever it stand, because our participation of Christ in His Sacrament dependeth on the co-operation of His omnipotent power which maketh it his Body and Blood to us; whether

* See infra, Part ii.

Hooker.

with change or without alteration of the elements, (such as they imagine) we need not greatly to care or require."*—*Ibid.* vi.

"Take therefore that wherein all agree, and then consider by itself what cause why the rest in question should not rather be left as superfluous than urged as necessary.—*Ibid.* vii.

Christ lifted up his hands and eyes to heaven at the institution of the Sacrament.

"Being assembled for no other cause which they could imagine, but to have eaten the Passover only that Moses appointed, when they saw their Lord and Master with hands and eyes lifted up to heaven, first

[* "Well," said they, "dost thou not think that his very natural body, flesh, blood, and bone, is contained under the Sacrament, and there present without all figure or similitude?" "No," said I, "I do not so think. *Notwithstanding I would not that any should count that I make my saying*, which is the negative, any article of faith. For even as I say, that you ought not to make any necessary article of the faith of your part (which is the affirmative), so I say again that we make no necessary article of the faith of our part, but leave it indifferent for all men to judge therein, as God shall open his heart, and no side to condemn or despise the other, but to nourish in all things brotherly love, and one to bear another's infirmity."—Fox's Acts and Monuments, t. i. 1034. And, p. 1035: "I will not hold it as an article of faith, but that you may without danger or damnation either believe it or think the contrary."—Epistle of Frithus.]

"Whereas popish doctrine doth hold that priests by word of consecration make the real, my whole discourse is to show that God by the Sacrament maketh the mystical body of Christ; and that seeing in this point as well Lutherans as Papists agree with us, which only point containeth the *benefit* we have of the Sacrament, it is but needless and unprofitable for them to stand the one upon consubstantiation, and upon transubstantiation the other, which doctrines they neither can prove, nor are forced by any necessity to maintain, but might very well surcease to urge them, if they did heartily affect peace, and seek the quietness of the Church."—Book V., ch. lxvi. vii., Hooker's M.S. note, Keble's Edit., vol. ii., 3rd ed., p. 354.]

bless and consecrate, for the endless good of all generations till the world's end, the chosen elements of Bread and Wine, which elements made for ever the instruments of life by virtue of His divine Benediction, they being the first that were commanded to receive from Him, the first which were warranted by His promise that not only unto them at the present time, but to whomsoever they and their successors after them did duly administer the same, those Mysteries should serve as conducts of life and conveyances of His Body and Blood unto them,—was it possible they should hear that voice, 'Take, eat, this is My Body; drink ye all of this, this is My blood;' possible that doing what was required and believing what was promised, the same should have present effect in them, and not fill them with a kind of fearful admiration at the heaven which they saw in themselves? They had at that time a sea of joy and comfort to wade in, and we, by that which they did, are taught that this heavenly food is given to us for the satisfying of our empty souls, and not for the exercising of our curious and subtile wits."

"If we doubt what those admirable words may import, let him be our teacher for the meaning of Christ to whom Christ was Himself a schoolmaster, let our Lord's Apostle be His interpreter, content we ourselves with his explication, My Body, *the Communion of My Body*, My Blood, *the Communion of My Blood*. Is there any thing more expedite, clear, and easy, than that as Christ is termed our Life because through Him we obtain life, so the parts of this Sacrament are His Body and Blood, for that they are so to us who receiving them receive that by them

marginal notes: Hooker. The elements made instruments of life by the Divine benediction.

<small>Hooker.</small>

which they are termed? The Bread and Cup are His Body and Blood, because they are causes instrumental, upon the receipt whereof the *participation* of His Body and Blood ensueth. For that which produceth any certain effect is not vainly nor improperly said to be that very effect whereunto it tendeth. Every cause is in the effect which groweth from it. Our souls and bodies quickened to eternal life are effects, the cause whereof is the Person of Christ; His Body and Blood are the true wellspring out of which this life floweth. So that His Body and Blood are in that very subject whereunto they minister life not only by effect or operation, even as the influence of the heavens is in plants, beasts, men, and in every thing which they quicken, but also by a far more divine and mystical kind of union, which maketh us one with Him even as He and the Father are one."—Book v. chap. lxvii. § 4, 5.

<small>The Sacrament confessed on all sides to be a real participation of Christ.</small>

"It is on all sides plainly confessed, first, that this Sacrament is a true and a real participation of Christ, who thereby imparteth Himself, even His whole entire Person, *as a mystical Head* unto every soul that receiveth Him, and that every such receiver doth thereby incorporate or unite himself unto Christ as *a mystical member of* Him, yea of them also whom He acknowledgeth to be His own; secondly, that to

<small>The Person of Christ communicated.</small>

whom *the Person of Christ* is thus communicated, to them He giveth by the same Sacrament His Holy Spirit to sanctify them as it sanctifieth Him who is their Head; thirdly, that what *merit, force, or virtue*

<small>The virtue of his sacrificed Body and Blood given by the Sacrament.</small>

soever there is in His sacrificed Body and Blood, we freely, fully, and wholly have it by this Sacrament; fourthly, that *the effect thereof in us is a real transmutation of our souls and bodies* from sin to righteousness, from death and corruption to immortality and life; fifthly, that because the Sacrament being of itself but a corruptible and earthly creature, must needs be thought an unlikely instrument to work so admirable effects in man, we are therefore to rest ourselves altogether upon *the strength of His glorious power*, Who is able and will bring to pass, that the Bread and Cup which He giveth us shall be truly the thing He promiseth.

"It seemeth therefore much amiss, that against them whom they term Sacramentaries, so many invective discourses are made, all running upon two points, that the Eucharist is not a bare sign or figure only, and that the efficacy of His Body and Blood is not all we receive in this Sacrament. For no man having read their books and writings which are thus traduced can be ignorant that both these assertions they plainly confess to be most true. They do not so interpret the words of Christ as if the name of His Body did import but the *figure* of His Body, and to *be* were only to *signify* His Blood.* They grant that

[* The circumstance of there being a real presence does not exclude a figurative presence also. It is only the doctrine of a merely figurative presence which is here condemned by Hooker. Pascal has the following observation on the same subject:

"Il y a un grand nombre de vérités, et de foi et de morale, qui semblent repugnantes et contraire, et qui subsistent toutes dans une ordre admirable. Nous croyons que la substance du pain étant changée en celle du corps de notre Seigneur Jésus Christ, il est présent réellement au saint Sacrement. Voilà une des vérités. Une autre est, que ce Sacrement est aussi une figure de la croix et de la gloire, et une commémoration des deux. Voilà la foi Catholique qui comprend ces deux vérités qui

<small>Hooker.</small>

<small>The Person of Christ in true and real though mystical manner communicated.</small>

these holy mysteries received in due manner do instrumentally both make us partakers of the grace of that Body and Blood which were given for the life of the world, and besides also impart unto us even in true and real though mystical manner the very Person of our Lord Himself, whole, perfect, and entire, as hath been showed."—Book v. chap. lxvii. § 7, 8.

" All three [Roman Catholics, Lutherans, and Calvanists] do plead God's omnipotency. . . . As evident it is how they teach that Christ is personally there present, yea, present whole, albeit a part of Christ be corporally absent from thence ; that Christ assisting this heavenly banquet with his personal and true presence, doth by his own divine power add to the natural substance thereof supernatural efficacy, which addition to the nature of those consecrated elements changeth them, and maketh them that unto us which otherwise they could not be ; that to us they are thereby made such instruments, as mystically yet truly, invisibly yet really, work our communion or fellowship with the Person of Jesus Christ, as well in that he is man as God. . . . . In a word, it appeareth not that of all the ancient Fathers of the Church any one did ever concur or

semblent opposées. L'hérésie d'aujourd' hui ne concevant pas que ce Sacrement contient tout ensemble, et la présence de Jésus Christ, et sa figure, et qu'il soit Sacrifice et commémoration de Sacrifice, croit qu'on ne peut admettre l'une de ces vérités, sans exclure l'autre. Par cette raison ils s'attachent à ce point, que ce Sacrement est figuratif, et en cela ils ne sont pas hérétiques. Ils pensent que nous excluons ce vérité, et de la vient qu'ils nous font tant d'objections sur les passages des Peres qui le disent. Enfin ils nient la Presence Réelle et en cela ils sont hérétiques."
—*Pensées*, xxviii. 4.]

imagine other than only a mystical participation of Christ's holy Body and Blood in the Sacrament, neither are their speeches concerning this change of the elements themselves into the Body and Blood of Christ such, that a man can thereby in conscience assure himself it was their meaning to persuade the world either of a corporal consubstantiation of Christ with these sanctified and blessed elements before we receive them, or of the like transubstantiation of them into the Body and Blood of Christ. Which both to our mystical communion with Christ are so unnecessary, that the Fathers who plainly hold but this mystical communion cannot easily be thought to have meant any other change of sacramental elements than that which the same spiritual communion did require them to hold."—*Ibid.* Hooker.

... " That which all parties receive for truth,—that which every one having sifted is by no one denied or doubted, must needs be matter of infallible certainty. Whereas, therefore, there are but three expositions made of ' This is my body.' The first, ' This is, in itself, before participation, *really and truly the natural substance of my body, by reason of the co-existence which my omnipotent body hath with the sanctified elements of bread,*' which is the Lutheran's interpretation. The second, ' This is in itself and before participation *the very true and natural substance of my body by force of that Deity which, with the words of consecration, abolisheth the substance of bread, and substituteth in the place thereof my body,*' which is the Popish construction. The last, '*This hallowed food, through concurrence of Divine power, is, in verity and truth, unto faithful receivers, instrumentally a cause of that mys-*

Hooker.*tical participation, whereby, as I make myself wholly theirs, so I give them in hand an actual possession of all such saving grace as my sanctified body can yield,*
No notice of Zuingli's opinion here.*and as their souls do presently need; this is* (to them and in them) *my body.*' Of these three rehearsed interpretations the last hath in it nothing but what the rest do all approve and acknowledge to be most true; nothing but that which the words of Christ are on all sides confessed to enforce; nothing but that which the Church of God hath always thought necessary; nothing but that which alone is sufficient for every Christian man to believe concerning the use and force of this Sacrament; finally, nothing but that wherewith the writings of all antiquity are consonant, and all Christian confessions agreeable. . . . In this, where they all speak but one thing, their discourses are heavenly, their words sweet as the honeycomb, their tongues melodiously tuned instruments, their sentences mere consolation and joy, are we not hereby almost, even with voice from heaven, admonished which we may safeliest cleave unto?

"He which hath said of the one Sacrament, 'Wash, and be clean,' hath said concerning the other likewise, 'Eat, and live.' If, therefore, without any such particular and solemn warrant as this is, that poor distressd woman coming unto Christ for health, could so constantly resolve herself, 'may I but touch the skirt of his garment I shall be whole,' what moveth us to argue of the manner how life should come by bread, our duty being here but to take what is offered, and most assuredly to rest persuaded of this, that can we but eat we are safe? When I behold with mine eyes some small and scarce discernible grain or seed whereof nature maketh a promise that a tree shall come, and when afterwards of that tree any skilful artificer undertaketh to frame some exquisite and curious work, I look for the event, I move no question about performance, either of the one or of the other. Shall I simply credit nature in things natural, shall I in things artificial rely myself on art, never offering to make doubt, and in that which is above both art and nature refuse to believe the Author of both, except He acquaint me with His ways, and lay the secret of His skill before me? Where God Himself doth speak those things which either for height and sublimity of matter, or else for secrecy of performance we are not able to reach unto, as we may be ignorant without danger, so it can be no disgrace to confess we are ignorant. Such as love piety will as much as in them lieth know all things that God commandeth, but especially the duties of service which they owe to God. As for His dark and hidden works, they prefer as becometh them in such cases simplicity of faith before that knowledge, which curiously sifting what it should adore, and disputing too boldly of that which the wit of man cannot search, chilleth for the most part all warmth of zeal, and bringeth soundness of belief many times into great hazard. Let it therefore be sufficient for me, presenting myself at the Lord's Table, to know what there I receive from Him, without searching or inquiring of the manner how Christ performeth His promise; let disputes and questions, enemies to piety, abatements of true devotion, and hitherto in this cause but over patiently heard, let them take their rest; let curious and sharp-witted

Hooker.

men beat their heads about what questions themselves will, the very letter of the word of Christ giveth plain security that these mysteries do as nails fasten us to His very Cross, that by them we draw out, as touching efficacy, force, and virtue, even the blood of His gored side, in the wounds of our Redeemer we there dip our tongues, we are dyed red both within and without, our hunger is satisfied and our thirst for ever quenched; they are things wonderful which he feeleth, great which he seeth, and unheard of which he uttereth, whose soul is possessed of this Paschal Lamb and made joyful in the strength of this new Wine, this Bread hath in it more than the substance which our eyes behold, this Cup hallowed with solemn benediction availeth to the endless life and welfare both of soul and body, in that it *The Eucharist a medicine for our souls and a sacrifice of thanksgiving.* serveth as well for a medicine to heal our infirmities and purge our sins as for a sacrifice of thanksgiving; with touching it sanctifieth, it enlighteneth with belief, it truly conformeth us unto the image of Jesus Christ. What these elements are in themselves it skilleth not, it is enough that to me which take them *So in Edward's First Book, "may be unto us the Body and Blood," ut fiant nobis corpus et sanguis.* they are the Body and Blood of Christ, His promise in witness hereof sufficeth, His word He knoweth which way to accomplish; why should any cogitation possess the mind of a faithful communicant but this, O my God, Thou art true, O my soul, thou art happy!"—Book v. chap. lxvii. § 12.*

" The power of the Ministry of God translateth out of darkness into glory; it raiseth man from the

[* This passage is almost a literal translation from the " Cœna Domini" of Arnoldus de Bonâ Villâ (a contemporary of St. Bernard), which was formerly attributed to St. Cyprian.]

earth, and bringeth God Himself down from heaven; by blessing visible elements it maketh them invisible grace; it giveth daily the Holy Ghost; it hath to dispose of that Flesh which was given for the life of the world, and that Blood which was poured out to redeem souls; when it poureth malediction upon the heads of the wicked, they perish; when it revoketh the same, they revive. O wretched blindness, if we admire not so great power; more wretched if we consider it aright, and notwithstanding, imagine that any but God can bestow it! To whom Christ hath imparted power, both over that mystical body which is the society of souls, and over that natural which is Himself, for the knitting of both in one (a work which antiquity doth call the making of Christ's Body) the same power, is, in such, not amiss both termed a kind of mark or character, and acknowledged to be indelible."—Book v. chap. lxxvii. § 1. *[Hooker. The power given for the making of Christ's body indelible.]*

"These holy mysteries received in due manner do instrumentally both make us partakers of the grace of that Body and Blood which were given for the life of the world, and besides also impart in true and real though mystical manner, the very Person of our Lord Himself, whole, perfect, and entire, as hath been showed."—*Ibid.* chap. lvii. *[The Person of Christ imparted by the Sacrament.]*

"Touching the sense of antiquity in this cause ... as evident it is how they teach that Christ is personally there present; yea, present whole, albeit a part of Christ be corporally absent from thence; that Christ, assisting this heavenly banquet with His personal and true presence, doth by His own divine power add to the natural substance thereof supernatural efficacy. Which addition to the nature of those con- *[A part of Christ corporally absent.]*

<small>Hooker.</small>

secrated elements changeth them, and maketh them that unto us which otherwise they could not be."—Book v. lxvii. § 11.

[There are other passsages in which Hooker uses the words "real presence," and the "body and blood of Christ" (as St. Augustine had done before), as synonymous with the *virtue* of the Sacrament, or of "the benefits of which we are partakers thereby;" as where he says that "the real presence of Christ's most holy Body and Blood" is "only to be found in the worthy receiver of the Sacrament," and "in the very heart and soul of him who receiveth."—Book V. c. 57. A more strictly dogmatic teaching was soon after introduced into the Church Catechism.]

JACKSON.

[Thomas Jackson, born 1579; DD. 1622; Dean of Peterborough; died in 1640.]

"All that are partakers of this Sacrament, eat Christ's Body and drink His Blood sacramentally: that is, they eat that Bread which sacramentally is His Body, and drink that Cup which sacramentally is His Blood, whether they eat or drink faithfully or unfaithfully. For *all the Israelites* (1 Cor. x.) *drank of the same spiritual rock, which was Christ* sacramentally: *all* of them were partakers of His presence, when Moses smote the rock. Yet, with '*many of them God was not well pleased,*' because they did not faithfully either drink or participate of His presence. And more displeased He is with such as eat Christ's Body and drink His Blood unworthily, though they eat and drink them sacramentally; for eating and drinking so only, that is, without faith, or due

<small>The wicked eat the Body and Blood of Christ sacramentally but not worthily.</small>

respect, they eat and drink to their own condemnation, because they do not discern, or rightly esteem, Christ's Body or Presence in the Holy Sacrament. *Jackson.*

"May we say then, that Christ is really present in the Sacrament, as well to the unworthy as to the faithful receivers? Yes, this we must grant, yet must we add withal, that he is really present with them in a quite contrary manner; really present He is, because virtually present to both; because the operation or efficacy of His Body and Blood is not metaphorical, but real in both. Thus the bodily sun, though locally distant for its substance, is really present by its heat and light, as well to sore eyes as to clear sights, but really present to both, by a contrary real operation; and by the like contrary operation, it is really present to clay and to wax, it really hardeneth the one, and really softeneth the other. So doth Christ's Body and Blood, by its invisible, but real influence, mollify the hearts of such as come to the Sacrament with due preparation; but harden such as unworthily receive the consecrated Elements. *The effect of Christ's Body and Blood on those who receive it unworthily.* If he that will hear the word, must take heed how he hears, much more must he which means to receive the Sacrament of Christ's Body and Blood, be careful how he receives. He that will present himself at this great marriage feast of the Lamb without a wedding garment, had better be absent. It was always safer, not to approach the presence of God manifested or exhibited in an extraordinary manner (as in His sanctuary or in the ark), than to make appearance before it in an unhallowed manner, or without due preparation. Now, when we say that Christ is really present in the Sacrament, our meaning is, that as *Christ's real presence in the Sacrament.*

<small>Jackson.</small> God He is present in an extraordinary manner, after such a manner as He was present (before His incarnation) in His Sanctuary the Ark of His Covenant; and by the power of His Godhead thus extraordinarily present, He diffuseth the virtue or operation of His human nature, either to the vivification or hardening of their hearts, who receive the Sacramental pledges."—Vol. iii. p. 333, 334.

DR. DONNE.

[John Donne, an eminent poet and divine, born 1553; Dean of St. Paul's in 1624; died 1631. See his life by Izaac Walton.]

"But yet, though this Bread be not so transubstantiated, we refuse not the words of the Fathers, in which they have expressed themselves in this mystery. Not *Irenæus* his '*est corpus*,' that that Bread is his Body now. Not Turtullian's '*fecit corpus*,' that that Bread is made his Body, which was not so before. Not St. Cyprian's '*mutatus*,' that that Bread is changed. Not Damascene's '*supernaturaliter mutatus*,' that that Bread is not only changed so in the use, as when at the king's table certain portions of bread are made bread of essay, to pass over every dish whether for safety or for majesty; not only so civilly changed, but changed supernaturally. No nor Theophylact's '*transformatus est*' (which seems to be the word that goes farthest of all), for this transforming cannot be intended of the outward form and fashion, for that is not changed, but be it of that internal form which is the very essence and nature of the Bread, so it is transformed, so the Bread hath received a new form, a new essence, a new nature, because whereas the nature of bread is but to nourish the body, the nature of this Bread now is to nourish the soul. And therefore *cum non dubitavit Dominus dicere, 'Hoc est Corpus Meum' cum signum daret corporis*, since Christ forbore not to say, 'This is My Body,' when He gave the sign of His body, why should we forbear to say of that Bread, This is Christ's Body, which is the sacrament of His Body?"—80 *Sermons.* ed. 1640, p. 37. 4th *Serm. on the Nativity.*

"This Sacrament of the Body and Blood of our Saviour, Luther calls safely, *Venerabile et adorabile*, for, certainly, whatsoever that is which we see, that which we receive is to be adored, for we receive Christ; He is *res Sacramenti*, the form, the essence, the soul of the Sacrament, *et Sacramentum sine re Sacramenti mors est*. To take the body and not the soul, the bread and not Christ, is death; but he that feels Christ in the receiving of the Sacrament, and will not bend his knee, would scarce bend his knee if he saw Him. The first of that royal family which thinks itself the greatest of Christendom at this day, the House of Austria, had the first marks of their greatness, the Empire, brought into that House, for a particular reverence done to the holy and blessed Sacrament.* What the bread and wine is, or what

[* "In an age of superstition, the piety of Rhodolph was pure and ardent, and he was punctual and devout in attending the services of the Church. . . . . .

"The contemporary chronicles, among numerous anecdotes, record an instance of his courteous demeanour towards the inferior clergy, and of his unfeigned respect for the forms of religion. Being engaged in hunting, he met between Fahr and Baden, a priest on foot, carrying the host to a sick person, and as the road

Donne. becomes of it, Damascene thinks too impertinent to be inquired. He thinks he hath said enough (and so really he has), *migrat in substantiam animæ.*"—Sermon 68, fol. 693.

ANDREWES.

[Lancelot Andrewes, born 1555; Chaplain to Queen Elizabeth, 1589; Dean of Westminster, 1601; Bishop of Chichester, 1605; Bishop of Ely, 1609; Bishop of Winchester, 1618; died 1626.]

"The Cardinal is not, unless 'willingly, ignorant,' that Christ hath said, 'This is My Body,' not 'This is My Body *in this mode.*' Now about the object we are both agreed; all the controversy is about the *mode.* The 'This is,' we firmly believe; that 'it is in this mode' (the Bread, namely, being transubstantiated into the Body), or of the mode whereby it is wrought, that 'it is,' whether *in,* or *with,* or *under,* or *transubstantiated,* there is not a word in the Gospel. And because not a word is there, we rightly detach it from being a matter of faith; we may place it amongst the decrees of the schools, not among the articles of faith. What Durandus is reported to have said of old (Neand. Synop. Chron., p. 203) we approve of. 'We hear the word, feel the effect, know not the manner, believe the Presence.' The Presence, I say, we believe, and that no less true than yourselves. Of the mode of the Presence, we

Margin notes: Hoc est corpus meum. Transubstantiation to be reckoned among the decrees of the schools. Durandus.

was extremely dirty, and the torrents swollen with rain, he alighted, and gave his horse to the priest, saying, it ill became him to ride, whilst the bearer of Christ's body walked on foot.— Vitorod Chron. Ann. Leob. in Pez. tom. i., Hager, &c."—History of the House of Austria, by the Ven. William Coxe, Archdeacon of Wilts. London, 1807. Vol. i. p. 63.]

define nothing rashly, nor, I add, do we curiously inquire; no more than how the Blood of Christ cleanseth us in our Baptism; no more than how in the Incarnation of Christ the human nature is united into the same Person with the Divine. We rank it among Mysteries (and indeed the Eucharist itself is a mystery), 'that which remaineth, ought to be burned with fire' (Ex. xii. 13), that is, as the Fathers elegantly express it, to be adored by faith, not examined by reason."—*Answer to Bellarmine*, c. i. p. 11.

<small>Andrewes.</small>

Again:—

"And I may safely say it with good warrant from those words especially and chiefly, which, as He Himself saith of them, are 'spirit and life,' even those words, which joined to the element make the blessed Sacrament.

<small>The words joined to the element make the Sacrament.</small>

"There was good proof made of it this day. All the way did he preach to them, even till they came to Emmaus, and their hearts were hot within them, which was a good sign; but their eyes were not opened but 'at the breaking of bread,' and then they were. That is the best and surest sense we know, and therefore most to be accounted of. There we taste, and there we see; 'taste and see how gracious the Lord is.' There we are made to 'drink of the Spirit,' there our 'hearts are strengthened and stablished with grace.' There is the Blood which shall 'purge our consciences from dead works,' whereby we may 'die to sin.' There the Bread of God, which shall endue our souls with much strength; yea, multiply strength in them to live unto God; yea, to live to Him continually; for he that 'eateth His flesh and

Andrewes. drinketh His blood, dwelleth in Christ, and Christ in him;' not inneth, or sojourneth for a time, but dwelleth continually. And never can we more truly or properly say *in Christo Jesu Domino nostro*, as when we come new from that holy action, for then He is in us, and we in Him indeed."—*Serm. I. on the Resurrection*, p. 204, 5.

"And again too, that to a many with us it is indeed so *fractio panis*, as it is that only and nothing besides ; whereas the 'Bread which we break is the partaking of Christ's true 'Body,'—and not of a sign, figure, or remembrance of it. For the Church hath ever believed a true fruition of the true Body of Christ in that Sacrament."—*Works*, vol. v. p. 66, 67.

"We believe a true Presence no less than you. The King (James I.) acknowledges that Christ is truly present and truly to be adored in the Sacrament, that is the *res Sacramenti*, and not the *Sacramentum*, the *earthly* part, as Irenæus calls it, the *visible*, as Augustine . . . . . We also with Ambrose adore the flesh of Christ in the mysteries; and not *it*, but Him who is worshipped on the altar. . . . . . . Nor do we eat the flesh without first adoring with Augustine. And yet we do not adore the Sacrament."[*]

[*] " Christus ipse Sacramenti res, in et cum Sacramento, extra et sine sacramento, ubi ubi est, adorandus est . . . Rex (Jacobus) Christum in Eucharistia vere *presentem*, vere et *adorandum* statuit, rem scilicet Sacramenti ; at non Sacramentum, *terrenam* scilicet partem, ut Irenæus ; *visibilem*, ut Augustinus. . . . Nos vero et *in mysteriis carnem Christi* adoramus cum Ambrosio : et non, *id*, sed Eum qui super altare colitur. Male enim, *quid ibi colatur*, quærit Cardinalis, cum *quis*, debuit : Cum Nazianzenus, *Eum* dicat, non *id*. Nec *carmen manducamus quin adoremus*

And again,—

"All witnesses testify in favour of mutation, immutation, transmutation, but there is no mention of *substantial*, or of substance. Nor do we deny the preposition *trans*, and we acknowledge the *elements* to be *transmuted*. But we seek in vain for *substantial*. Nor do we deny that the elements are changed by the benediction, so that the consecrated bread is not that which nature has formed, but that which the benediction has consecrated, and even changed by consecration. And we believe, with [Gregory] Nyssen, *that the nature of the bread and wine was changed*, but neither he nor we to be *transubstantiated*." *

From the Royal Declaration prefixed to

THE ARTICLES OF RELIGION,

A.D. 1628.

". . . That for the present, though some differences have been ill raised, yet we take comfort in this, that all clergymen within our realm have always most wil-

prius, cum Augustino. Et Sacramentum tamen nulli adoramus."—(Ad. Card. Bellarmin. Apolog. Oxford ed. 1851, p. 26, 7.)

* "Testes vero omnes, pro mutatione, immutatione, transmutatione, loquuntur. Substantialis autem ibi, vel substantiæ, mentio nulla. At et nos præpositionem ibi *trans* non negamus: et *transmutari elementa* damus. *Substantialem* vero quærimus, nec reperimus usquam.

" . . . Neque nos, elementum benedictione mutari, contradicimus: ut panis jam consecratus *non sit panis, quem natura formavit; sed quem benedictio consecravit*, et consecrando etiam immutavit. . . . . Et nos cum Nysseno credimus, *virtute benedictionis, panis et vini naturam immutari*, nec tamen vel ipse, vel nos, *transubstantiari*."—*Ibid.* p. 262, 3.

_{Royal Declaration.} ingly subscribed to the Articles established; which is an argument to us, that they all agree in the true, usual, literal meaning of the said Articles; and that even in those curious points, in which the present differences lie, men of all sorts take the Articles of the Church of England to be for them; which is an argument again, that none of them intend any desertion of the Articles established."

ARTICLES RELATING TO THE SACRAMENTS.
A.D. 1562.

"ART. XXV.

Of the Sacraments.

... The Sacraments were not ordained of Christ to be gazed upon or be carried about, but that we should duly use them. And in such only as worthily receive the same, they have a wholesome effect or operation, but they that receive them unworthily, purchase to themselves damnation, as S. Paul saith."

"ART. XXV.

De Sacramentis.

Sacramenta non in hoc instituta sunt a Christo, aut spectarentur aut circumferrentur sed ut rite illis uteremur, et in his duntaxat, qui digne percipiunt, salutarem habent effectum : qui vero indigne percipiunt, damnationem (ut inquit Paulus) sibi ipsis acquirunt."

"ART. XXVIII.

Of the Lord's Supper.

The Supper of the Lord is not only a sign of the

"ART. XXVIII.

De Cœna Domini.

Cœna Domini non est tantum signum mutuæ

love that Christians ought to have among themselves one to another; but rather is a Sacrament of our Redemption by Christ's death: insomuch that to such as rightly, worthily, and with faith, receive the same, the Bread which we break is a partaking of the Body of Christ; and likewise the Cup of Blessing is a partaking of the Blood of Christ.

Transubstantiation, or (the change of the substance of bread and wine) in the Supper of the Lord, cannot be proved by holy Writ; but is repugnant to the plain words of Scripture, overthroweth the nature of a Sacrament, and hath given occasion to many superstitions.

The body of Christ is given, taken, and eaten,

benevolentiæ Christianorum inter sese, verum potius est sacramentum nostræ per mortem Christi redemptionis. Atque adeo rite, digne, et cum fide sumentibus, panis quem frangimus est communicatio corporis Christi: similiter poculum benedictionis est communicatio sanguinis Christi. Panis et vini transubstantiatio in Eucharistia ex sacris literis probari non potest; sed apertis Scripturæ verbis adversatur, sacramenti naturam evertit, et multarum superstitionum dedit occasionem.

Corpus Christi datur, accipitur, et manducatur in cœna tantum cælesti et spirituali ratione. Medium autem, quo corpus Christi accipitur* et manducatur in cœna, fides est.

* ["Bossuet says that this assertion of the Article is certainly true, provided the reception be understood of a *useful* reception, in the sense of S. John speaking of Jesus Christ: 'His own received him not, though he was in the midst of them;' *i. e.* they did not receive his doctrine nor his grace.—*Variat.* x. sect. vi." Palmer on the Church, vol. i. p. 530.]

Article XXVIII. in the Supper, only after an heavenly and spiritual manner. And the mean whereby the body of Christ is received and eaten in the Supper is Faith.

The Sacrament of the Lord's Supper was not by Christ's ordinance reserved, carried about, lifted up, or worshipped."*

Sacramentum Eucharistiæ ex institutione Christi non servabatur, circumferebatur, elevebatur, nec adorabatur.

* [The following was the original form of the article in 1552:—

Forasmuch as the truth of man's nature requireth that the body of one and the self-same man cannot be at one time in several places; but must needs be in one certain place, therefore the body of Christ cannot be present at one time in many and divers places; and because, as Holy Scripture doth teach, Christ was taken up into heaven, and there shall continue until the end of the world, a faithful man ought not either to believe or openly confess the real bodily presence, as they term it, of Christ's flesh and blood in the Sacrament of the Lord's Supper.

Quum naturæ humanæ veritas requirat, ut unius ejusdemque hominis corpus in multis locis simul esse non posset, sed in uno aliquo et definito loco esse oportet; idcirco Christi corpus in multis et diversis locis eodem tempore præsens non esse potest. Et quoniam, ut tradunt scripturæ, Christus in cœlum fuit sublatus, et ibi usque ad finem sæculi est permansurus, non debet quisquam fidelium carnis ejus et sanguinis realem et corporalem (ut loquunter), præsentiam in Eucharistia vel credere vel profiteri.

The articles of 1552 were never ratified, but those on the Sacraments are, with the exceptions here given, the same with those ratified in 1562.

"The design of the Government," says Burnet, "was at that time much turned to the drawing over the body of the nation to the

"ART. XXIX.	"ART. XXIX.
Of the wicked which eat not the Body of Christ in the use of the Lord's Supper.	*De manducatione corporis Christi et impios illud non manducare.*
The wicked, and such as be void of a lively faith,	Impii, et fide viva destituti [licet carnaliter et

Reformation, in whom the old leaven had gone deep, and no part of it deeper than the belief in the corporal presence of Christ in this Sacrament; therefore it was not thought expedient to offend them by so particular a definition in this matter, in which the very word *real presence* was rejected." (Art. xxviii.)

Dr. Lingard (the historian) thus observes upon the sense of this article. "I shall perhaps be told that these and similar passages [in the Church Catechism] should be explained by the 28th article, which clearly shows in what sense the Church of England understands the real presence. I think, however, that from the cautious manner in which that article is worded, an argument may be deduced in favour of Catholic doctrine. The words are, ' The body of Christ is given, taken, and eaten in the Supper, only after a heavenly and spiritual manner.' Be it so. [Roman] Catholics say as much. But does this heavenly and spiritual manner[1] prevent it from being the real body that was broken, and the real blood that was shed for us? If so, that which is taken and received in the Sacrament may be the influence of Christ's Body and Blood, the graces which he has purchased for us, the title to a heavenly inheritance, or anything else that it may please the ingenuity of our adversaries to suggest, but it certainly is not the inward part or thing signified which, according to the Catechism, is the real Body and the real Blood of Christ. But if, on the contrary, this spiritual manner does not exclude the reality of the Body and Blood of Christ, then my former argument remains in all its force. And here I may observe, that the article says more than the Catechism. It says that the Body of Christ is *given*, as well as taken and eaten, in the Lord's Supper. As the action of giving

---

[1] [The words, "spiritual and heavenly manner," "cœlesti et spirituali ratione," are nearly those of St. Augustine, "Comedite spiritualiter panem cœlestem," where he applies "cœlestem" to the object, and "spiritualiter" to the subject.]

Article XXIX. [although they do carnally and visibly press with their teeth] (as Saint *Augustine* saith) [the Sacrament of the Body and Blood of Christ], yet in no wise are they partakers of Christ: but rather, to their condemnation, do eat and drink the sign or Sacrament of so great a thing."*

visibiliter] (ut Augustinus loquitur) [corporis et sanguinis Christi sacramentum dentibus premant] nullo tamen modo Christi participes efficiuntur.

Sed potius tantæ rei Sacramentum seu symbolum ad judicium sibi manducant et bibunt."

is prior to that of taking and eating, the Body of Christ must exist in the Sacrament before it is taken and eaten by the communicant. 'The means by which it is taken and eaten is faith.' But by what means is it *given?* On this head the article is silent, and, I think with some reason, for it cannot be given by faith. To exercise an act of faith 'is to eat Christ,' and, undoubtedly, to eat, and to give to another to eat, are two very different things.

"The same doctrine, of really *giving* in the Sacrament the Body and Blood of Christ to the faithful, I find in Dean Nowell's Catechism for Schools, first published in 1570, '*Corpus et sanguis Christi fidelibus in Cœna Domini* præbentur, ab illisque accipiuntur, comeduntur, et bibuntur, cœlesti tantum et spirituali modo, vere tamen atque reipsa.' "—*Tracts*, p. 553.]

* [This article appears to be directed against such as held that "the wicked and those that be devoid of a lively faith," do not receive to their *condemnation* the Sacrament of the Body and Blood of Christ. The contrast is between two classes of persons,—those who are partakers of Christ, *i. e.* the faithful and penitent, and those who receive to their condemnation, *i. e.* the wicked and unfaithful. The article says nothing of those who hold that the Body and Blood of Christ are received by the wicked to their *condemnation*. It is clear that by the *partaking of Christ* a beneficial reception of the Sacrament is intended, and no other is contemplated by the terms employed. The persons condemned by the Article are those described in the Homily, who

consider the Sacrament to operate as a charm, even in the case of those "devoid of a lively faith" or who "think that without faith we may enjoy the eating and drinking thereof, or that that is the fruition of it," which "is but to dream of a gross carnal feeding;" in the same Homily the Sacrament is compared to "physic provided for the body," which "being misused, more hurteth than profiteth.—1 Cor. xi."—*First part of the Homily concerning the Sacrament.* <small>Article XXIX.</small>

The following is the passage of St. Augustine here referred to: "Ac per hoc, qui non manet in Christo, et in quo non manet Christus, proculdubio nec manducat carnem ejus, nec bibit ejus sanguinem. Sed magis tantæ rei Sacramentum ad judicium sibi manducat et bibit."—*Hom. on John* vi. 5, 6. <small>The wicked do not eat the Flesh of Christ</small>

The passage of the xxixth Article included in brackets, p. 55, 56, is found in Bede and Alcuin, as well as in some manuscripts and printed editions of St. Augustine's works, but is rejected by the Benedictine editors as an interpolation.[1] It is more correct as given in the xxixth Article than it is in the Roman Breviary. The sentiment here expressed by Augustine, which is identical with that in the xxixth Article, seems at first view to countenance the notion that in no way whatever do the wicked receive the body and blood of Christ; but an examination of the context of St. Augustine will show that it was the subjective presence he had in view, or what he otherwise calls the spiritual reception. That St. Augustine held an objective presence of Christ in the Sacrament is abundantly clear from many passages in his writings, including the Tract from which this passage is adduced by our Reformers: "So many who eat that flesh and drink that blood with a false heart, or who, after having eaten and drunk become apostates, do they abide in Christ, or Christ in them? But there is, undoubtedly, a certain manner of eating that flesh and drinking that blood, in which way who shall have eaten and drunk, he abides in Christ and Christ in him. Wherefore, not in what way soever a man shall have eaten the flesh of Christ, and drunk the blood of Christ, does Christ abide in him and he in Christ, but in a certain way, which way he had in view, when he spake these words. In fine, he now expoundeth how that is effected which he saith, and what it is to eat His Body and drink His Blood. 'He that eateth <small>Except with a false heart.</small> <small>He that eateth Christ's flesh dwelleth in Christ.</small>

---

[1] [See *infra*, p. 108, note on Thorndike.]

my flesh and drinketh my blood [John vi. 56] dwelleth in me and I in him.' And therefore who dwelleth not in Christ, and in whom Christ dwelleth not, without doubt doth neither eat his flesh nor drink his blood, but rather to his own condemnation doth eat and drink the sacrament of so great a thing." And in a former part of the same discourse, he observes: "The sacrament of this thing, that is, of the Body and Blood of Christ, in some places every day, in some places at certain intervals of days, is on the Lord's Table prepared, and from the Lord's Table is taken; by some to life, by some to destruction; but the *thing*, (res ipsa) of which it is the sacrament, is for every man to life, for none to destruction.

"Many ate manna and died not. Why? Because that visible food they spiritually understood, spiritually hungered after, spiritually tasted, that they might spiritually be filled. For we too at this day do receive visible food; but the Sacrament is one thing, the *virtue* of the Sacrament is another. How many receive from the altar and die, yea, by receiving die? whence the Apostle saith, he eateth and drinketh judgment to himself. It was not that the sop of the Lord was poison to Judas. And yet he received it, and when he received it, the enemy entered into him; not that he received any evil thing, but that he being evil did in evil wise receive what was good. Look to it then, brethren, eat ye spiritually the heavenly bread, bring innocence to the altar.

"This then is the bread that cometh down from heaven, that whoso eateth thereof may not die. But this in regard to the virtue of the Sacrament, not in regard of the visible Sacrament; he that eateth inwardly, not outwardly; he that eateth in the heart, not he that presseth with his teeth.

"Let all this, I say, hereunto avail us, that we eat not the flesh and blood of Christ only in the Sacrament; which do also many evil men, but that even unto the participation of the Spirit we do eat and drink; yea, though many in the present time, do, together with us, eat and drink *temporally* the Sacraments, who shall have in the end eternal torments.

"Prepare not thy teeth, but thy heart."[1] "Why make ready thy teeth and thy belly? Believe, and thou hast eaten."[2] "Spiritually understand what I have spoken to you. You are not to eat that

---

[1] De verbis Domini. Serm. 33, t. v. p. 566.
[2] Johan. Tract. 25, tom. iii. p. 11, 487.

Body which you see, nor drink that Blood which they will shed who will crucify me. I have commended to you a Sacrament. Spiritually understood, it will quicken you. Though it must be visibly celebrated, yet it must be invisibly understood.[1]

"What you see is the Bread and Cup, which even your eyes inform you; what your faith requires to be informed,—the bread is the Body of Christ, the cup his Blood. . . . How is the Bread his Body and the cup, or what it contains, his Blood? These things, brethren, are therefore called Sacraments, because in them one thing is seen, another understood. What appears has a bodily form; what is understood has a spiritual fruit."— *Serm.* 272, *ad Infantes*, t. v. part 1, p. 1103. "The Body and Blood of Christ will then be life to each, if what is visibly seen in the Sacrament, be in actual verity, *spiritually* eaten, *spiritually* drunk."—*Serm.* 2, *de Verbis Apost.* t. v. part 1, p. 64.

Many passages may be adduced from St. Augustine's writings to show that he entertained a clear notion of the objective sense, although he uses expressions which will bear a different meaning, and although Calvin professed to follow him. He does not, it is admitted, always clearly distinguish between the *res sacramenti* and the *virtus sacramenti*, whereas it would be more consistent to identify the first with the inward part or thing signified, the second with its effect on the devout soul. This latter is what our liturgy calls 'spiritually eating the flesh of Christ,' the soul being in this case brought into spiritual relation with Him.

The following are an example of the passages to which we refer:

"The rich approach the Lord's Table, and receive his Body and Blood, but they worship only, they are not fed, because they do not imitate." (Epist. cxl. s. 66.)

"As Judas, to whom the Lord gave the sop, gave place to the Devil, not by receiving an evil thing, but by receiving in an evil manner, so every one who receives unworthily the Lord's Sacrament does not make it an evil thing, because he himself is evil, nor because he does not receive it to salvation, does he receive nothing. For it was the Body and Blood of the Lord, notwithstanding, to them to whom the Apostle said, 'He that eateth and drinketh unworthily, eateth and drinketh judgment to himself.' Corpus enim Domini et sanguuis Domini nihilominus erat etiam illis quibus dicebat apostolus, qui manducat indigne,

---

[1] In Ps. xclii. t. iv. p. 1066.

Article XXIX.

judicium sibi manducat et bibit."—*De Baptism. contra Donatist.* lib. v. c. 8. See *supra*, p. 26. On another accasion the same Father observes, in regard to Judas, that he ate "the bread of the Lord," while the other disciples ate "the Lord who was bread." In Johan. lix. 1. And, contrasting their case with that of the heretics, he asserts, in his 'City of God,' that the 'Catholics eat the Body of Christ not only in the Sacrament, but in reality' (non solo sacramento sed reipsa manducant corpus Christi).—P. 639.

Theodoret, however, held that the substance of the bread remained after consecration.

Many of the Fathers, who clearly maintain an objective presence, as Theodoret, *infra*, make use, upon certain occasions, of expressions of the same import with those cited in the XXIXth. Article from Augustine, of which the following are examples:

St. Hilary: "Panis qui de cœlo descendit, non nisi ab eo accipitur, qui Dominum habet et Christi membrum est."—*De Trin.* lib. viii.

Prosper: "Qui discordat a Christo nec carnem ejus manducat nec sanguinem bibit."—*Senten.* 339.

Jerome: "Those who are lovers of pleasure more than lovers of God, neither eat his Body nor drink his Blood." (Omnes voluptatis amatores magis quam Dei .... nec comedunt carnem Jesu nec bibunt sanguinem ejus." In Isai. lxvi.) And "Polluimus panem, *i. e.* Corpus Christi, quando indigni accedimus ad altare et sordidi mundum sanguinem bibimus." In Malach. i.

St. Ambrose: "Ille accipit qui seipsum probat."—*De Bened. Patriarch.* c. 9.

St. Leo: "Ore Indigno Christi corpus accipiunt." Ser. iv. de Quadrages.

Finally, Origen (in Matt. xv.) asserts that "the wicked cannot eat the word made flesh," yet, notwithstanding his spiritualizing tendencies, he observes upon another occasion in addressing the unprepared, "you do not fear to approach the Eucharist, and to partake of the Body of Christ, as if you were pure and clean."—(In Psalmos, Hom. ii. 6. See also Hom. xiii.).

And Theodoret: "He gave his Body and Blood not only to the eleven apostles, but to the traitor."—In 1 Cor. xi.

Even Strauss allows that the primitive Christians believed in an objective presence in the Sacrament. "In the view of the writers of the gospels (and after their example in that of the earliest Fathers) the Bread in the Lord's Supper *was* the Body of Christ. But if they had been asked whether the substance of the Bread was *changed*, they would have replied in the negative ; if they had been told that the communicants partook of the Body *with and under* the form of Bread, they would not have understood it ; if it had been asserted that the Bread only *signified* the Body, they would not have been satisfied." Leben Jesu. Vol. ii. Conf. Baumgarten-Crusius ii.—*Wilson on the Lord's Supper.* Cleaver's ed. p. 203.]

THE GOLDEN CANONS.

" Certi quidam articuli de sacro ministerio et procuratione Ecclesiarum, in quos plene consensum est in Synodo a Domino Matthæo Archiepiscopo Cantuar, et totius Angliæ Primate et Metropolitano et reliquis omnibus ejus Provinciæ Episcopis, partim personaliter præsentibus, partim procuratoria manu subscribentibus in Synodo inchoata Londini in æde Divi Pauli, 3 die April, 1571."

Concionatores.

" Imprimis vero videbunt, ne quid unquam doceant pro concione, quod a populo religiose teneri et credi velint, nisi quod consentaneum sit doctrinæ veteris aut novi testamenti, quodque ex illa ipsa doctrina Catholici Patres, et veteres Episcopi collegerint. Et quoniam articuli illi religionis Christianæ in quos consensus est ab Episcopis in legitima et sancta synodo, jussu atque authoritate serenissimæ Principis Elizabethæ convocata, et celebrata, hauddubie collecti sunt ex sacris libris veteris et novi testamenti et cum cœlesti doctrina, quæ in illis continetur, per omnia congruunt, quoniam etiam liber publicarum precum, et liber de inauguratione Archiepiscopum, Episcoporum Presby-

The Golden Canons. terorum et Diaconorum, nihil continent ab illa ipsa doctrina alienum, quicunque mittentur ad docendum populum, illorum articulorum authoritatem et fidem, non tantum concionibus suis, sed etiam subscriptione confirmabunt. Qui secus fecerit et contraria doctrina populum turbaverit, excommunicabitur."

"And the preacher was in his exposition appointed to observe the CATHOLIC interpretation of the old Doctors of the Church, as we may see in the nineteenth canon of the sixth Council of Constantinople held in Trullo. The canon is this: 'Let the governors of churches every Sunday at the least, teach their clergy and people the oracles of piety and true religion; collecting out of Divine Scripture, the sentences and doctrines of truth, not transgressing the antient bounds and traditions of the holy Fathers. And if any doubt or controversy arise about Scripture, let them follow that interpretation which the lights of the Church and the doctors have left in their writings. By which they shall more deserve commendation, than by making private interpretations, which if they adhere to, they are in danger to fall from the truth.' To this agrees the canon made in Queen Elizabeth's time, A.D. 1571. 'The preachers chiefly shall take heed that they teach nothing in their preaching which they would have the people religiously to observe and believe, but that which is agreeable to the doctrine of the Old Testament and the New, and that which the Catholic Fathers and ancient Bishops have gathered out of that doctrine.' These GOLDEN CANONS, had they been duly observed, would have been a great preservative of truth, and the Church's peace."—*Sparrow's Rational. Com. Prayer*, p. 202.

Canon of 1571.

PRAYER BOOK OF THE CHURCH OF IRELAND.

Church of Ireland.

From the Form for reconciling Converts from the Church of Rome.*

"*In the receiving of priests, or such as are likely to teach others, it will be necessary to add this clause opposed to the former, the last clause of Pius Quartus his profession of faith.*

"I promise by diligent reading, attending to and studying the Holy Scriptures in the translation of the Church of England, together with the writings of the pure and more uncorrupt Fathers, especially of the three first centuries, to endeavour to attain the perfect knowledge of the whole body of Christian truth; nor will I ever hold, teach, or maintain what I am not persuaded in my heart is agreeable to the Holy Scriptures, interpreted by the joint consent of the said Fathers, so far as I can discover them. So help me God."

The Scriptures as interpreted by the joint consent of the Fathers.

THE PROTESTATION.

"This was first added in the second book of King Edward, in order to disclaim any adoration to be intended by that ceremony—[kneeling at the Sacrament of the Lord's Supper]—either unto the Sacramental bread and wine there bodily received, or unto any real or essential presence there being of Christ's natural flesh and blood. But upon Queen

The Sacramental bread and wine not to be adored.

* [This Form was drawn up by the learned Dr. Anthony Dopping, Bishop of Kildare, and afterwards of Meath, and formerly Fellow of Trinity College, Dublin, and was first printed in 4to, Dublin, 1690, and annexed to the Book of Common Prayer.]

The Protestation.

Elizabeth's accession this was laid aside. For it being the Queen's design . . . . to unite the nation as much as she could in one faith, it was therefore recommended to the Divines to see that there should be no definition made against the aforesaid notion, but that it should remain as a speculative opinion not determined, but in which every one might be left to the freedom of his own mind. And being thus left out, it appears no more in any of our Common Prayers till the last review, at which time it was again added . . . . excepting that the words *real and essential* Presence were thought proper to be changed for *corporal* Presence. For a real* presence of the body and blood of Christ in the Eucharist is what our Church frequently asserts in this very office of Communion, in her Articles, in her Homilies, and her Catechism, particularly in the two latter."†

Real and essential Presence.

* [At the last revision the terms of this Protestation were altered in favour of the real presence *in* the Sacrament.

† [The following is the Protestation referred to, as it appears in the later editions of the second Book of Edward (to which it was added after the book had been ratified by Parliament) compared with it as altered at the last revision. This was formerly known as the *black rubric*.

"Although no order can be so perfectly devised, but it may be of some, either for their ignorance or infirmity, or else of malice and obstinacy, misconstrued, depraved, and interpreted in a wrong part. And yet because brotherly charity willeth that, so much as conveniently may be, offences should

BISHOP OVERALL.

[John Overall, born 1559; Fellow of Trinity College, Cambridge, 1596; Regius Professor of Divinity, and Master of Catherine Hall; Dean of St. Paul's, 1601; Prolocutor of the Lower House, 1603; Bishop of Lichfield and Coventry, 1614; Norwich, 1618; died, 1619. He had the character among his contemporaries of being the best scholastic divine in the English nation. Bishop Cosin describes him as "Vir undique doctissimus, et omni encomio major."]

"*So to eat the Flesh of Thy dear Son Jesus Christ, and to drink His Blood.*] By this it may be known what our Church believeth, and teacheth of the Presence of Christ's Body and Blood in the Sacrament.

be taken away, therefore we were willing to do the same. Whereas, it is ordained in the book of Common Prayer, in the administration of the Lord's Supper, that the communicants kneeling should receive the holy Communion: which thing being well meant for a signification of the humble and grateful acknowledging of the benefits of Christ given to the worthy Receiver, and to avoid the profanation and disorder which about the holy Communion might else ensue: but yet the same kneeling might be thought or taken otherwise, we do declare that it is not meant thereby that any adoration is done, or ought to be done, either unto the sacramental bread or wine there

"Whereas it is ordained in this Office for the Administration of the Lord's Supper, that the communicants should receive the same kneeling: (which order is well meant, for a signification of our humble and grateful acknowledgment of the benefits of Christ *therein* given to all worthy Receivers, and for the avoiding of such profanation and disorder in the holy Communion, as might otherwise ensue;) yet, lest the same kneeling should by any persons, either out of ignorance and infirmity, or out of malice and obstinacy, be misconstrued and depraved; it is hereby declared, That thereby no adora-

F

Overall. And though our new masters would make the world believe she had another mind, yet we are not to follow their private fancies, when we have so plain and so public a doctrine as this."

bodily received, or to any real[1] or essential presence there being of Christ's natural Flesh and Blood. For as concerning the sacramental bread and wine, they remain still in their very natural substances, and therefore may not be adored, for that were idolatry to be abhorred of all faithful Christians. And as concerning the natural Body and Blood of our Saviour Christ, they are in heaven and not here. For it is against the truth of Christ's true natural Body to be in more places than in one at one time."

tion is intended, or ought to be done, either unto the Sacramental Bread or Wine there bodily received, or unto any Corporal Presence of Christ's natural Flesh and Blood. For the Sacramental Bread and Wine remain still in their very natural substances, and therefore may not be adored; (for that were Idolatry to be abhorred of all faithful Christians;) and the natural Body and Blood of our Saviour Christ are in Heaven, and not here; it being against the truth of Christ's natural Body to be at one time in more places than one."

---

[1] [" If ye understand by this word *really*," observes Cranmer, "*corporaliter, i. e.* corporally, so that by the body of Christ is understood a *natural* body and *organical*—so, the first proposition doth vary, not only from the usual speech and phrase of Scripture, but also is clean contrary to the Holy Word of God and Christian profession, when as both the Scripture doth testify by these words, and also the Catholic Church hath professed from the beginning, Christ to have left the world, and be set at the right hand of the Father till He comes to judgment."]—*Works*, iv. 11, 12.

* [Thomas Aquinas, Summa, part. iii. quæst. 75, art. 1, in reference to this question observes:—"It is objected that a *body* cannot be at once in many places, since this is not compatible even to the nature of angelic beings; for in this case, it might be omnipresent. Now, the Body of Christ is a true body, and is in

"That we receiving these Thy creatures of Bread and Wine, &c., may be partakers of His blessed Body and Blood.] [That] together with the hallowed elements of the Bread and Wine, we may receive the Body

Overall.

heaven—therefore it cannot be truly in the Sacrament of the altar; but only by way of a figure, or as in a sign." On which he observes:—" The Body of Christ is not in such a manner in this Sacrament as is a body in a place, which body is by its dimensions commensurate with a place, but in a special mode, peculiar to this Sacrament. Whence we say that the Body of Christ is on different altars, not as in different places, but as in a Sacrament, by which we do not understand that Christ is there as in a mere sign, although Sacraments are of the nature of signs, but we understand that the Body of Christ is present here in a manner peculiar to this Sacrament."

"The saying of Augustine, "The Lord is above until the end of the world, but yet the truth of the Lord is with us here below, for the body in which He rose from the dead must abide in one place, while its truth is everywhere diffused," and other similar passages, are to be understood of the Body of Christ as it appears in its proper form (according to which the Lord himself says, Matt. xxvi., " Me ye have not always "), it is however invisibly present under the forms of this Sacrament, wherever the Sacrament is exhibited.

"The fourth objection proceeds from the notion of the presence of the Body of Christ, as if present after the manner of a *Body*, that is in its visible form, and does not apply to it as it is present *spiritually*, that is, invisibly and by the power of the Spirit."

The following is the entire of the original passage from Aquinas:—

" Ad secundum dicendum, quod verbum illud Augustini 'Donec sæculum finiatar, sursum est Dominus, sed tamen et hic nobiscum est veritas Domini; corpus enim in quo resurrexit, in uno loco oportet esse, veritas autem ejus ubique diffusa est,' et omnia similia, sunt intelligenda de corpore Christi secundum quod videtur in propriâ specie (secundum quod etiam ipse Dominus dicit, Matt. xxvi., Me autem non semper habebitis), invisibiliter tamen sub speciebus hujus sacramenti est, ubicunque hoc sacramentum perficitur.

<small>Overall.</small> and Blood of Christ, which are truly exhibited in this Sacrament, the one as well as the other.

"These words, as I once conferred with a Papist, were mightily excepted against, because forsooth they must acknowledge no Bread and Wine, but a desition of the nature and being of both. My answer was, that here we term them so before consecration; after that we call them so no more, but abstain from that name, because our thoughts might be wholly taken up with the spiritual food of Christ's Body and Blood. So in the Thanksgiving following we say, *That hast vouchsafed to feed us who have duly received these holy Mysteries, with the spiritual food of the most precious Body and Blood of Thy Son,* &c. In the meanwhile we deny not the Bread and Wine to remain there still as God's creatures. And I wonder the Papists should so contend for this same *desitio panis et vini,* whenas, in their own service or mass, they abstain not from these words, THY CREATURES, after consecration, as we do. See the book, PER QUEM OMNIA DOMINE BONE CREAS! A certain argument that the Church of Rome never meant to

---

"Ad tertium dicendum, quod Corpus Christi non est eo modo in hoc Sacramento sicut corpus in loco, qui suis dimensionibus loco commensuratur, sed quodam speciali sive spirituali modo, qui est proprius huic sacramento, unde dicimus, quod Corpus Christi est in diversis altaribus, non sicut in diversis locis, sed sicut in hoc Sacramento. Per quod non intelligimus, quod Christus sit ibi solum sicut in signo, licet Sacramentum sit in genere signi, sed intelligimus Corpus Christi hic esse (sicut dictum est) secundum modum proprium huic sacramento.

"Ad quartum dicendum, quod ratio illa procedit de præsentia corporis Christi, prout est præsens per modum corporis, id est in sua specie visibili, non autem prout est spiritualiter, id est invisibili modo, et virtute spiritus."—(*Summa* iii, 9, 75, a. 1.)]

teach that doctrine, which private men, the late doctors and schoolmen, have brought up and propagated."—*Additional Notes to the Book of Common Prayer. Appendix to Nicholls.*

Overall.

"*These holy Mysteries with the spiritual food of the most precious Body and Blood, &c.*] Before consecration we called them God's creatures of Bread and Wine, now we do so no more after consecration... though the bread remain there still, to the eye.... And herein we follow the Fathers, who after consecration would not suffer it to be called Bread and Wine any longer, but the Body and Blood of Christ.

"*Very Members Incorporate.*] So Cyril. in Catech. Myst. 4. *Sumpto Corpore et Sanguine Christi ait nos fieri* συσσώμους, *i. e. ejusdem Corporis cum Christo, et inter nos* συναίμους, *i. e., ejusdem Sanguinis.*

"*And be also heirs through hope.*] So the ancient Fathers were wont to prove the article of our resurrection by the nature of this very Sacrament. They use this reason to exhort the people unto the frequent receiving of the Holy Communion; because they say it is, φάρμακον ἀθανασίας, *Medicamentum Immortalitatis et Antidotum* τὸ μὴ θανεῖν. *An antidote not to die;* which if the men of this age would but set their hearts on, as they did, we should not have them set so slightly by the Sacrament as they do."

"*And if any of the Bread and Wine.*] It is confessed by all Divines that upon the words of the consecration, the Body and Blood of Christ is really and substantially present, and so exhibited and given to all that receive it, and all this not after a physical and sensible, but after an heavenly and incomprehensible manner. But there yet remains this controversy

The Body and Blood really and substantially present after consecration.

Overall. among some of them, whether the Body of Christ be present only in the use of the Sacrament, and in the act of eating, and not otherwise. They that hold the affirmative, as the Lutherans (in Confess. Sax.) and all Calvinists, do seem to me to depart from all antiquity, which places the presence of Christ in the virtue and benediction used by the Priest, and not in the use of eating the Sacrament. And this did most Protestants grant and profess at first.

"*What is the inward part or thing signified?*] I cannot see where any real difference is betwixt us about this Real Presence, if we could give over the study of contradiction, and understand one another aright."—*Catechism.*

"In the Sacrament of the Eucharist, or the Lord's Supper, the Body and Blood of Christ, and therefore the whole of Christ is verily and indeed present, and is verily partaken by us, and verily combined with the Sacramental signs, as being not only significative but exhibitory; so that in the Bread duly given and received the Body of Christ is given and received; in the Wine given and received, the Blood of Christ is given and received; and thus there is a communion of the whole of Christ in the communion of the Sacrament. . . . ."—*Ibid.*

["Probably," observes Mr. Alexander Knox (*Remains*, vol. ii.), "had Bishop Overall lived before the tenth century, he would have thought he had sufficiently stated his belief, in the above expressions; but placed as he was in other circumstances, it was expedient for him not only to maintain ancient truth, but to protest against erroneous innovation: he therefore added these words:—]

"Yet not in any bodily, gross, earthly manner, as by transubstantiation, or consubstantiation, or any like devices of human reason, but in a mystical, heavenly, and spiritual manner, as is rightly laid down in our Articles." (*As quoted and translated in Knox's Remains*, vol. ii. p. 163.) *Overall.*

Again,

"There are certain zealots who condemn the practice of our Church in receiving the sacrament of the Body and Blood of Christ kneeling, or at least object to His worship and reservation." (Morem ecclesiæ nostræ sacramentum corporis et sanguinis Christi de geniculis accipiendi oppugnant, aut eum saltem colere et custodire recusant.)—*Epist. Præstant. Virorum, Epist.* 290.—*Overall's Letter to Grotius, idib. August.* 1617. *Reservation and worship*

CHURCH CATECHISM.

"How many Sacraments hath Christ ordained in his Church?—Two only, as generally necessary to salvation, that is to say, Baptism, and the Supper of the Lord.

What meanest thou by this word Sacrament?—I mean an outward and visible sign of an inward and spiritual grace given unto us, ordained by Christ himself, as a means whereby we receive the same, and a pledge to assure us thereof.

How many parts are there in a Sacrament?—Two; the outward visible sign, and the inward spiritual grace.

What is the outward visible sign or form in Bap-

Church Catechism.

tism?—Water, wherein the person is baptized in the name of the Father, and of the Son, and of the Holy Ghost.

What is the inward and spiritual grace?—A death unto sin, and a new birth unto righteousness: for being by nature born in sin, and the children of wrath, we are hereby made the children of grace.

What is required of persons to be baptized?—Repentance, whereby they forsake sin; and faith, whereby they stedfastly believe the promises of God made to them in that Sacrament.

Why then are infants baptized, when by reason of their tender age they cannot perform them?—Because they promise them both [repentance and faith] by their sureties; which promise, when they come to age, themselves are bound to perform.

Why was the Sacrament of the Lord's Supper ordained?—For the continual remembrance of the sacrifice of the death of Christ, and of the benefits which we receive thereby.

What is the outward part or sign of the Lord's Supper?—Bread and Wine, which the Lord hath commanded to be received.

What is the inward part, or thing signified?—The Body and Blood of Christ, which are verily and indeed taken and received by the faithful in the Lord's Supper.

What are the benefits whereof we are partakers thereby?—The strengthening and refreshing of our souls by the Body and Blood of Christ, as our bodies are by the Bread and Wine."

Bishop Overall.

"The Church Catechism being afterwards thought

defective as to the doctrine of the Sacraments, King James I. appointed the Bishops to add a short and plain explanation of them, which was done accordingly in the most excellent form we see, being penned by Bishop Overall, then of St. Paul's, and allowed by the Bishops."—*Wheatly on the Common Prayer*, chap. viii. s. 1.

Church Catechism.

THE HOMILIES.

[The first Book of Homilies was issued in 1547, 1st Edward; the second, 1st Elizabeth, said in Art. XXIV. to "contain a godly and wholesome doctrine, and necessary for these times." Their authors are not all known. Some are said to be Cranmer's, that on "Christian Love and Charity," is by Bonner, some are supposed to be Jewell's, and others translations from the Latin.]

"Before all other things, this we must be sure of especially, that this Supper be in such wise done and ministered as our Lord and Saviour did and commanded to be done, as His Holy Apostles used it, and the good Fathers in the primitive Church frequented it. For as that worthy man, St. Ambrose, saith, he is unworthy of the Lord that otherwise doth celebrate that mystery than it was delivered by Him."—*First part of the Homily of the worthy receiving of the Sacrament.*

"Justinus Martyr, who lived about one hundred and sixty years after Christ, saith thus of the administration of the Lord's Supper in his time:— "Upon the Sunday, assemblies are made, both of them that dwell in cities, and of them that dwell in the country also,—amongst whom, as much as may

Justin Martyr.

Homilies. be, the writings of the Apostles and Prophets are read. Afterwards, when the reader doth cease, the chief minister maketh an exhortation, exhorting them to follow honest things. After this we rise all together and offer prayers ; which being ended as we have said, bread and wine and water are brought forth ; then the head minister offereth prayers and thanksgiving with all his power, and the people answer, Amen."—*Justinus Martyr, Apol.* 2. *Homily of Common Prayer and Sacraments.*

[St. Justin had just observed :—]

The consecrated bread the flesh and blood of Jesus. "We do not receive these things as common bread or common drink, but, as our Saviour Jesus Christ being made incarnate by the word of God, had both flesh and blood for our salvation, so we are taught that the food over which thanks have been given by the prayer of the word which came from Him—(whereby through conversion our flesh and blood are nourished)—is both the flesh and blood of the incarnate Jesus."*—*Ibid.*]

Hoc est corpus meum. "Neither need we to think that such exact knowledge is required by every man, that he be able to discuss all high points in the doctrine thereof; but thus much we must be sure to hold, that in the Supper of the Lord there is no vain ceremony, no bare sign, no untrue figure of a thing absent. (Matt. xxvi.) But, as the Scripture saith, the Table of the Lord, the bread and cup of the Lord, the memory of Christ, the annunciation of His death, yea, the communion of the Body and

---

* [In reference to this passage Mr. Harold Brown observes, that "Justin Martyr held high Eucharistic doctrine," and that "it is evident he was no Zuinglian."—Article xxviii.]

Blood of the Lord, in a marvellous incorporation, which, by the operation of the Holy Ghost (the very bond of our conjunction with Christ), is through faith wrought in the souls of the faithful, whereby not only their souls live to eternal life, but they surely trust to win to their bodies a resurrection to immortality. (1 Cor. x.) The true understanding of this fruition and union, which is betwixt the body and the head, betwixt the true believers and Christ, the ancient Catholic fathers, both perceiving themselves, and commending to their people, were not afraid to call this Supper, some of them, the salve of immortality and sovereign preservative against death; other, a deifical communion; other, the sweet dainties of our Saviour; the pledge of eternal health; the defence of faith; the hope of the resurrection; other, the food of immortality, the healthful grace, and the conservatory to everlasting life. *Iren. lib. iv. cap. 34; Ignat. Epist. ad Ephes. Dionysius, Origen, Optat.; Cyp. de Cœna Domini; Atha. de Pec. in Spir. Sanct.* All which sayings, both of the holy Scripture and godly men, truly attributed to this celestial banquet and feast, if we would often call to mind, Oh! how would they inflame our hearts to desire the participation of these mysteries, and oftentimes to covet after this bread; continually to thirst for this food! Not as especially regarding the terrene and earthly creatures which remain; but always holding fast and cleaving by faith to the Rock, whence we may suck the sweetness of everlasting salvation."—*The first part of the Homily concerning the Sacrament.*

Homilies.

1 Cor. x.

Calix benedictionis quam benedicimus.

Homilies. "So that at this His table we receive not only the outward Sacrament, but the spiritual thing also; not the figure but the truth; not the shadow only, but the body, not to death, but to life"—*Ibid.*

Basil. "Wherefore," saith Basil, "it behoveth him that cometh to the Body and Blood of Christ, in commemoration of Him that died and rose again, not only to be pure from all filthiness of the flesh and spirit, lest he eat and drink his own condemnation, but also to show out evidently a memory of Him that died and rose again for us, in this point, that ye be mortified to sin and world," &c. *De Bap.* lib. i. c. 3. So then we must show outward testimony in following the signification of Christ's death: amongst the which this is not esteemed the least, to render thanks to Almighty God for all His benefits, briefly comprised in the death, passion, and resurrection of His dearly beloved Son. The which thing, because we ought chiefly at this table to solemnize, the godly Fathers named it *Eucharistia*, that is, thanksgiving: as if they should have said, Now, above all other times, ye ought to laud and praise God. . . . Seeing then that the name and thing itself doth monish us of thanks, let us, as St. Paul saith, offer always to God the host or sacrifice of praise by Christ, that is, the fruit of the lips, which confess His name." Heb. xiii. For as David singeth, *He that offereth to God thanks and praise honoureth Him.* Ps. i.—*Second part of the Homily concerning the Sacrament.*

Christ's Body and Blood received under the form of bread and wine. "Hereafter shall follow Sermons . . . of the due receiving of His blessed Body and Blood, under the form of bread and wine."—*Notice at the end of the First Book of Homilies.*

"Deserve not the heavy and dreadful burthen of God's displeasure for thine evil will towards thy neighbour, so unreverently to approach to this Table of the Lord."—*Chrysostom, ad pop. Ant. Hom. vi.* —*Ibid.* {Homilies.}

"And shall we think that the wretched and sinful person shall be excusable at the Table of the Lord?" —*Ibid.*

". . . For surely if we do not with earnest repentance cleanse the filthy stomach of our soul, it must needs come to pass that . . . so shall we eat this wholesome bread and drink this cup to our eternal destruction."—*Ibid.*

"Whereby we may perceive that we ought to purge our own souls from all uncleanness, iniquity, and wickedness, lest when we receive the mystical bread, as Origen saith, we eat it in an unclean place, that is, in a soul defiled and polluted with sin." *Ibid.*

"When a great number of the Israelites were overthrown in the wilderness, Moses, Aaron, and Phineas, did eat manna, and pleased God; for that they understood, saith St. Augustine, the visible meat *spiritually*. Spiritually they hungered it; spiritually they tasted it, that they might be spiritually satisfied. In Johan. Hom. vi. And truly as the bodily meat cannot feed the outward man, unless it be let into a stomach to be digested, which is healthful and sound; no more can the inward man be fed, except his meat be received into his soul and heart, sound and whole in faith. Therefore, saith St. Cyprian (*De Cœna Domini*) when we do these things, we need not whet our teeth; but with sincere faith we break and divide

Homilies. that whole bread. It is well known that the meat we seek for in this Supper is spiritual food; the nourishment of our soul, a heavenly refection and not earthly; an invisible meat and not bodily; a ghostly substance and not carnal; so that to think that without faith we may enjoy the eating and drinking thereof, or that that is the fruition of it, is but to dream of a gross carnal feeding, basely objecting and binding ourselves to the elements and creatures. Whereas by the advice of the Council of Nicene, we ought to lift up our minds by faith, and leaving these inferior and earthly things, there seek it where the Sun of righteousness ever shineth. *Concilium Nicen.* Take then, this lesson, O thou *(Eusebius, Bishop of Emissa, died about 360.)* that art desirous of this Table, of Emissenus, a godly Father, that when thou goest up to the reverend communion, to be satisfied with spiritual meats, thou look up with faith upon the holy Body and Blood of thy God, thou marvel with reverence; thou touch it with the mind, thou receive it with the hand of thy heart, and thou take it fully with thy inward man." *Euseb. Emis. Serm. de Euchar.*—*First part of the Homily concerning the Sacrament.*

* [Eusebius Emissenus, the same Father here cited, also observes, if the works attributed to him be genuine, "Invisibilis sacerdos visibiles creaturas in substantiam corporis et sanguinis sui verbo suo secreta potestate convertit, dicens, 'Accipite et edite, Hoc est corpus meum,' et sanctificatione repetitâ, 'Accipite et bibite, Hic est sanguis meus.'" (*Hom. Paschal.* v.) See Part ii.

"Quando benedicendæ verbis cœlestibus creaturæ sacris altarbus imponuntur, antequam invocatione sancti nominis consecrantur, substantia illic est panis et vini, post verba autem Christi, corpus est et sanguis Christi.

"Ecce Sacerdos in æternum secundum ordinem Melchisedek

"Basilius Magnus and Johannes Chrysostomus did in their time prescribe public orders of public administration, which they call Liturgies, and in them they appointed the people to answer to the prayers of the minister sometime *Amen;* sometime Lord have mercy upon us; And with Thy spirit; and We have our hearts lifted up unto the Lord," &c.—*Homily of Common Prayer and Sacraments.*

[The Homilist proceeds to prove from these Liturgies that the public prayers of the Church were in a language understood by the people.]

[The following is extracted from the Form of Consecration in the Liturgies of St. Chrysostom and Basil here referred to:—]

[*After the recitation of the words of Institution.*]

"O Son of God, who hast offered thyself to the Father as a sacrifice for our reconciliation, and art distributed to us as the bread of life, we pray Thee by the effusion of Thy divine Blood, have pity on the people whom Thou hast redeemed at so vast a price. We beseech Thee, O merciful God, send down upon

panem et vinum virtute ineffabili in sui corporis et sanguinis substantiam convertit. Sicut enim tunc vivebat et loquebatur, et tamen a discipulis comedebatur et videbatur: ita et modo integer et incorruptus manet et à fidelibus suis in panis et vini sacramento quotidie bibitur et manducatur. Nisi enim panis et vinum in ejus carnem et sanguinem verterentur, nunquam Ipse corporaliter manducaretur et biberetur. Mutantur enim ista in Illa, comeduntur et bibuntur Illa in istis; quod qualiter fiat Ipse solus novit qui omnia potest et omnia novit. Dixit enim tunc per se, dixit et modo per suos ministros, 'Hoc est corpus meum,' et tanta est ejus verbi virtus et efficacia, ut statim fiat quod dicitur."—*Homil.* lxii. *in ramis palmorum.*]

_{Homilies.} us, and upon these gifts, Thy co-eternal and consubstantial Holy Spirit, by which this blessed bread may become truly the Body of our Lord Jesus Christ, and this cup the Blood of our Lord Jesus Christ, changing* them by the Holy Spirit. That they be to the partakers, for the purifying of the soul, the forgiveness of sins, and the communication of the Holy Spirit, to the fulness of the kingdom of heaven."

[This form is common to all the Oriental Liturgies.]

[*After Communion.*]

"Let us who have received the precious Body and Blood of Christ, give thanks to him that hath dignified us with the participation of His holy mysteries, and let us request that it may not be to our condemnation, but to our salvation."—*Liturgy of St. Basil.*

HERBERT.

[George Herbert, born 1593; Fellow of Trinity College, Cambridge, 1619; Public Orator of the University; Prebendary of Layton Ecclesiæ, 1626; Rector of Bemerton, 1630; died, 1632. "Between George Herbert and Dr. Donne," observes Izaac Walton, "there was a long and dear friendship."]

* * * * *
But the holy men of God such vessels are
As serve Him up, who all the world commands,
When God vouchsafeth to become our food,
Their hands convey Him, who conveys their hands.
O what pure things, most pure must those things be,
   Who bring my God to me.
     The Priesthood.

---

* Μεταβαλὼν, mistranslated *transubstantiating* in a recent Roman Catholic work.—*Pascal, Liturgie Catholique.*

> "Come ye hither all, whose taste
>   Is your waste;
> Save your cost and mend your fare.
> God is here prepared and drest,
>   And the feast
> God, in whom all dainties are.
>
> Come ye hither all, whom wine
>   Doth define,
> Naming you not to your good,
> Weep what you have drunk amiss,
>   And drink this
> Which before you drink, is blood."
>
>   "THE INVITATION.

"The country parson, having to administer the sacrament, is at a stand with himself, how or what behaviour to assume for so holy things. Especially at communion time he is in great confusion, as being not only to receive God, but to break and administer Him. Neither finds he any issue in this, but to throw himself down at the throne of grace, saying, Lord, Thou knowest what Thou didst, when Thou appointedst to be done thus, therefore do Thou fulfil what Thou didst appoint, for Thou art not only the feast, but the way to it."—(*Priest to the Sacrament.*)

BISHOP TAYLOR.

[Jeremy Taylor, son of a barber at Cambridge; born 1613; entered a sizer 1626; afterwards Fellow. Chaplain to Archbishop Laud; Fellow of All Souls, Oxford, 1636; Bishop of Down, 1660; died, 1667. It has been said of him that "he

Taylor.

had the good humour of a gentleman, the eloquence of an orator, the fancy of a poet, the acuteness of a schoolman, the profoundness of a philosopher, the wisdom of a chancellor, the sagacity of a prophet, the reason of an angel, and the piety of a saint."]

The bread Christ's body.

But still bread.

"*After supper, Jesus took the bread and blessed it,* and made it to be a heavenly gift; He gave them *bread,* and told them it was *his body;* that body which was broken for redemption of man, for the salvation of the world. St. Paul calls it [bread] even after consecration: *The bread which we break, is it not the communication of the body of Christ?* So that by Divine faith we are taught to express our belief of this mystery in these words; [The bread, when it is consecrated and made sacramental, is the body of our Lord; and the fraction and distribution of it is the communication of that body, which died for us upon the cross.] He that doubts of either of the parts of this proposition must either think Christ was not able to verify his word, and to make *bread* by his benediction to become to us to be *his body,* or that St. Paul did not well interpret and understand this mystery when he called it *bread.* Christ reconciles them both, calling himself *the bread of life;* and if we be offended at it, because it is *alive,* and therefore less apt to become *food,* we are invited to it because it is *bread;* and if the Sacrament to others seems less mysterious because it is *bread,* we are heightened in our faith and reverence, because it is *life:* the bread of the Sacrament is the life of our soul, and the body of our Lord is now conveyed to us by being the bread of the Sacrament. And if we consider how easy it is to faith, and how impossible it seems to curiosity, we shall be taught confidence and modesty, a resigning our understanding to the voice of Christ and his Apostles, and yet expressing our own articles as Christ did, in indefinite significations. And possibly it may not well consist with our duty to be inquisitive into the secrets of the kingdom, which we see by plain events hath divided the Church almost as much as the Sacrament hath united it, and which can only serve the purposes of the school, and of evil men, to make questions for that, and factions for these, but promote not the ends of a holy life, obedience, or charity.

"Some so observe the literal sense of the words that they understand them also in a natural. Some so alter them by metaphors and preternatural significations, that they will not understand them at all in a proper way. We see it, we feel it, we taste it, and we smell it to be bread; and by philosophy we are led into a belief of that substance whose accidents these are, as we are to believe that to be fire which burns, and flames, and shines. But Christ also affirmed concerning it, *This is my body*; and if faith can create an assent as strong as its object is infallible, or can be as certain in its conclusions as sense is certain in its apprehensions, we must at no hand doubt but that it is Christ's body. Let the sense of that be what it will, so that we believe those words, and (whatsoever that sense is which Christ intended) that we no more doubt in our faith than we do in our sense, and then our faith is not reproveable. It is *hard* to do so much violence to our *sense* as not to think it *bread;* but it is more *unsafe* to do so much violence to our *faith* as not to believe it to be Christ's

Taylor. Body.* But it would be considered that no interest of religion, no saying of Christ, no reverence of opinion, no sacredness of the mystery is disavowed, if we believe both what *we hear* and what *we see*. He that believes it to be *bread*, and yet *verily* to be *Christ's Body*, is only tied also by implications to believe God's omnipotence, that he who affirmed it can also verify it. And they that are forward to believe the change of substance can intend no more, but that it be believed verily to be the Body of our Lord. And if they think it impossible to reconcile its being bread with the verity of being Christ's Body, let them remember that themselves are put to more difficulties, and to admit of more miracles, and to contradict more sciences, and to refuse the testimony of sense, in affirming the special manner of transubstantiation. And therefore it were safer to admit the words in their first sense, in which we shall no more be at war with reason, nor so much with sense, and not at all with faith. And for persons of the contradictory persuasion, who to avoid the natural sense, affirm it only to be figurative, since their design is only to make this Sacrament to be Christ's Body in the sense *of faith*, and not *of philosophy*, they may remember that its being really present does not hinder, but that all that reality may be spiritual; and if it be Christ's Body, so it be not affirmed such in a natural sense and manner, it is still only the object of faith and spirit; and if it be affirmed only to be spiritual, there is then no danger to faith in admitting the words of Christ's institution,

* " [Thus Luther declared that he would rather take the blood only with the Pope than the wine only with Zuingli.]"

This is my Body. I suppose it to be a mistake to think whatsoever is real must be natural, and it is no less to think spiritual to be only figurative; that is too much, and this is too little; philosophy and faith may well be reconciled, and whatsoever objection can invade this union may be cured by modesty. And if we profess we understand not the manner of this mystery, we say no more but that it is a mystery; and if it had been necessary we should have construed it into the most latent sense, Christ himself would have given a clavis, and taught the Church to unlock so great a secret. Christ said, *This is my Body; this is my Blood.* St. Paul said, *The bread of blessing that we break is the communication of the Body of Christ, and the chalice which we bless is the communication of the Blood of Christ.* And, *We are all of one body, because we eat of one bread.* One proposition as well as the other is the matter of faith, and the latter of them is also, of sense; one is as literal as the other; and he that distinguishes in his belief, as he may place the impropriety upon which part he please, and either say, it is improperly called *bread,* or improperly called *Christ's Body,* so he can have nothing to secure his proposition from error, or himself from boldness, in decreeing concerning mysteries against the testimonies of sense, or beyond the modesty and symplicity of Christian faith. Let us love and adore the abyss of Divine wisdom and goodness, and entertain the Sacrament with just and holy receptions, and then we shall receive all those fruits of it, which an earnest disputer or a peremptory dogmatiser, whether he happen right or wrong, hath no warrant to expect upon the interest of his opinion.

Taylor.

Taylor.

Christ's power shown in the Sacrament.

"In the institution of this Sacrament Christ manifested, first, his Almighty power; secondly, his infinite wisdom; and thirdly, his unspeakable charity. First, his power* is manifest in making the symbols to be instruments of conveying himself to the spirit of the receiver; He nourishes the soul with bread, and feeds the body with a sacrament; He makes the body spiritual by his graces there ministered, and makes the spirit to be united to his body by a participation of the Divine nature. In the Sacrament that body which is reigning in heaven is exposed upon *the table of blessing*, and his body which was broken for us is now broken again, and yet remains impassable. Every consecrated portion of bread and wine, does exhibit Christ entirely to the faithful receiver, and yet Christ remains one, while He is wholly ministered in ten thousand portions; so long as we call these mysterious, and make them intricate to exercise our faith, and to represent the wonder of the mystery, and to increase our charity, our being inquisitive into the abyss can have no evil purposes. God hath instituted the right in visible symbols to make the

---

* " [When Transubstantiation (or other such definition of the mode of Christ's presence in the Eucharist) is denied in the Church of England, it is not on the principle of its being impossible to omnipotence, but on other grounds, such as its being not reconcilable with Scripture, Catholic tradition, or the doctrine of the Primitive Church, its contradicting the nature of a Sacrament, &c. Thus Bishop Forbes (de Euchar. 1, 2): 'Many Protestants too boldly and dangerously deny that God has power to transubstantiate the bread into the Body of Christ;' and Bishop Marsh (Lecture iv.) observes that the 'miraculous conversion' implied by Transubstantiation, 'had it been *necessary*, lay, undoubtedly, within reach of *almighty* power.']"

secret grace as presential and discernible as it might, that by an instrument of sense our spirits might be accommodated as with an exterior object to produce an eternal act. But it is the prodigy of a miraculous power by instruments so easy to produce effects so glorious; this then is the object of *wonder* and *adoration.*"—*Life of Christ.* {Taylor.}

"It was happy with Christendom, when she, in this article, retained the same simplicity which she always was bound to do in her manners and intercourse; that is, to believe the thing heartily, and not to inquire curiously; and there was peace in this article for almost a thousand years together; and yet that transubstantiation was not determined, I hope to make very evident; 'In synaxi transubstantiationem serò definivit ecclesia: diù satis erat credere, sive sub pane consecrato, sive quocunque modo adesse verum Corpus Christi;' so said the great Erasmus: 'It was late before the Church defined transubstantiation; for long time together it did suffice to believe, that the true Body of Christ was present, whether under the consecrated bread or any other way:' so the thing was believed, the manner was not stood upon. And it is a famous saying of Durandus: 'Verbum audimus, motum sentimus, modum nescimus, præsentiam credimus:' 'We hear the word, we perceive the motion, we know not the manner, but we believe the Presence;' and Ferus of whom Sixtus Senensis affirms that he was 'vir nobiliter doctus, pius et eruditus,' hath these words: 'Cum certum sit ibi esse Corpus Christi, quid opus est disputare, num panis sub-

{The mystery to be believed, not curiously inquired into.}

{Transubstantiation late defined.}

stantia maneat, vel non?' 'When it is certain that Christ's Body is there, what need we dispute whether the substance of bread remain or no;' and therefore Cuthbert Tonstal, Bishop of Duresme, would have every one left to his conjecture concerning the manner: 'De modo quo id fieret, satius erat curiosum quemque relinquere suæ conjecturæ, sicut liberum fuit ante Concilium Lateranum:' 'Before the Lateran Council, it was free for every one to opine as they pleased, and it were better it were so now.' —But St. Cyril would not allow so much liberty; not that he would have the manner determined, but not so much as thought upon. 'Firmam fidem mysteriis adhibentes, nunquam in tam sublimibus rebus, illud *quomodo*, aut cogitemus aut proferamus.' For if we go about to think it or understand it, we lose our labour. 'Quomodo enim id fiat, ne in mente intelligere nec linguâ dicere possumus, sed silentio et firmâ fide id suscipimus:' 'We can perceive the thing by faith, but cannot express it in words, nor understand it with our mind," said St. Bernard. 'Oportet igitur (it is at last, after the steps of the former progress, come to be a duty), nos in sumptionibus divinorum mysteriorum, indubitatam retinere fidem, et non quærere quo pacto.' The sum is this: The manner was defined but very lately: there is no need at all to dispute it; no advantages by it; and therefore it were better it were left at liberty to every man to think as he please, for so it was in the Church for above a thousand years together; and yet it were better men would not at all trouble themselves concerning it; for it is a thing impossible to be understood; and therefore it is not fit to be inquired after."—*Real Presence*, vol. ix. p. 421—23. Heber's ed.

"This may suffice for the word 'real,' which the English Papists much use, but, as it appears, with much less reason than the sons of the Church of England: and when the Real Presence is denied, the word 'real' is taken for 'natural,' and does not signify 'transcendenter,' or in his just and most proper signification. But the word 'substantialiter' is also used by Protestants in this question, which I suppose may be the same with that which is in the Article of Trent, 'Sacramentaliter præsens Salvator substantiâ suâ nobis adest,' 'in substance, but after a Sacramental manner:' which words, if they might be understood in the sense in which the Protestants use them, that is really, truly, without fiction or the help of fancy, but 'in rei veritate,' so, as Philo calls spiritual things ἀναγκαιόταται οὐσίαι, 'most necessary, useful, and material substances,' it might become an instrument of a united confession."* . . . .—*Ibid.* p. 427.

"One thing more I am to note in order to the same purposes; that, in the explication of this question, it is much insisted upon, that it be inquired

---

* [The following is the definition of the Tridentine Council of the words "sacramentaliter" and "spiritualiter."

"Quoad usum autem recte et sapienter Patres nostri tres rationes hoc sanctum sacramentum accipiendi distinxerunt. Quosdam enim docuerunt sacramentaliter duntaxat id sumere, ut peccatores; alios tantum spiritualiter, illos nimirum qui voto propositum illum cœlestem panem edentes, fide vivâ quæ per dilectionem operatur, fructum ejus et utilitatem sentiunt; tertios porro sacramentaliter simul et spiritualiter."—*Sess.* xiii. *de Euchar. c.* viii.]

Taylor.

whether, when we say we believe Christ's Body to be 'really' in the Sacrament, we mean, 'that Body, that Flesh, that was born of the Virgin Mary,' that was crucified, dead, and buried? I answer, I know none else that He had, or hath: there is but one Body of Christ, natural, and glorified; but he that says, that Body is glorified, which was crucified, says it is the same Body, but not after the same manner: and so it is in the Sacrament; we eat and drink the Body and Blood of Christ, that was broken and poured forth; for there is no other body, no other blood, of Christ; but though it is the same which we eat and drink, yet it is in another manner: and, therefore, when any of the Protestant divines, or any of the fathers, deny that Body which was born of the Virgin Mary, that which was crucified, to be eaten in the Sacrament,—as Bertram, as St. Jerome, as St. Clemens Alexandrinus, expressly affirm; the meaning is easy;—they intend it is not eaten in a natural sense; and then calling it 'corpus spirituale,' the word 'spiritual' is not a substantial predication, but is an affirmation of the manner, though, in disputation it be made the predicate of a proposition, and the opposite member of a distinction. 'That Body which was crucified, is not that Body that is eaten in the Sacrament,'—if the intention of the proposition be to speak of the eating it in the same manner of being; but 'that Body which was crucified, the same Body we do eat,'—if the intention be to speak of the same thing in several manners of being and operating: and this I noted, that we may not be prejudiced by words, when the notion is certain and easy: and thus far is the sense of our doctrine in this article."—*Ibid.* 430.

Bertram. Jerome. Clemens Alex. Ridley.

"When the holy man stands at the table of blessing and ministers the rite of consecration, then do as the angels do, who behold and love and wonder that the Son of God should become food to the souls of His servants. That He who cannot suffer any change or lessening, should be broken into pieces, and enter into the body to support and nourish the spirit, and yet remain in heaven, while He descends to thee upon earth; that He who hath essential felicity should become miserable and die for thee, and then give himself to thee for ever to redeem thee from sin and misery; that by his wounds He should procure health to thee, by his affronts he should entitle thee to glory, by his death He should bring thee to life, and by becoming a man He should make thee partaker of the divine nature.

" . . . These are such glories, that although they are made so obvious that each eye may behold them, yet they are also so deep that no thought can fathom them; but so it hath pleased Him to make these mysteries to be sensible, because the excellence and depth of the mercy is not intelligible; that while we are ravished and comprehended within the infiniteness of so vast and mysterious a mercy, yet we be as sure of it as anything we see and feel, and smell and taste; but yet it is so great that we cannot understand it.

"These holy mysteries are offered to our senses, but not to be placed under our feet; they are sensible, but not common; and, therefore, as the weakness of the elements adds wonder to the excellence of the Sacrament, so let our reverence and venerable usage of them add honour to the elements, and acknow-

<small>Taylor.</small> ledge the glory of the mystery, and the divinity of the mercy. Let us receive the consecrated Elements with all devotion and humility of body and spirit, and do this honour to it, that it be the first food we eat, and the first beverage we drink that day . . . . and that your body and soul be prepared for its reception with abstinence from secular pleasures, that you may better have attended fastings and preparatory prayers."

"In the act of receiving, exercise acts of faith with much confidence and resignation, believing it not to be common bread and wine, but holy in their use, holy in their signification, holy in their change, holy in their effect; and believe, if thou art a worthy communicant, thou dost as verily receive Christ's Body and Blood to all effects and purposes of the spirit, as thou dost receive the blessed Elements with thy mouth, that thou puttest thy finger to his hand, and thy hand into his side, and thy lips to his fountain of blood, sucking life from his heart (*Cyprian. de Cœn. Dom.*); and yet, if thou dost communicate <small>Christ eaten by the unworthy, but to their death.</small> unworthily, *thou eatest and drinkest Christ to thy danger, and death, and destruction.* Dispute not concerning the secret of the mystery, and the nicety of the manner of Christ's presence . . . . . indefinitely assent to the words of institution, and believe that Christ, in the holy Sacrament, gives thee His Body and His Blood. He that believes not this, is not a Christian. He that believes so much needs not to inquire further, nor to entangle his faith by disbelieving his sense."—*Holy Living*, sect. x. p. 270, 271.

"No man must dare to approach to the Holy

Sacrament of the Lord's Supper if he be in a state of any one sin . . . *and he that receiveth Christ into an impure soul or body*, first turns his most excellent nourishment into poison, and then feeds upon it."—*Ibid.* p. 267.

<small>Taylor. Christ received into an impure soul.</small>

"Place thyself upon thy knees in the devoutest and humblest posture of worshippers, and think not much in the lowest manner to worship the King of men and angels, the Lord of Heaven and Earth, the great Lover of Souls, and the Saviour of the Body, Him whom all the angels of God worship, Him whom thou confessest worthy of all, and whom all the world shall adore, and before whom they shall tremble at the Day of Judgment. For if Christ be not there after a peculiar manner, whom or whose body do we receive? But if He be present, not in mystery only, but in blessing also, why do we not worship? But all the Christians always did so from time immemorial. 'No man eats this flesh unless he first adores,' said St. Austin, 'for the wise men and barbarians did worship this Body in the manger, with very much fear and reverence. Let us, therefore, who are citizens of heaven, at least not fall short of the barbarians. But thou seest him not in the manger, but on the altar. And thou beholdest Him not in the Virgin's arms, but represented by the Priest, and brought to thee in sacrifice by the Holy Spirit of God.' So S. Chrysostom argues, and accordingly this reverence is practised by the Churches of the East, and West, and South, by the Christians of India, by all the Greeks, as appears in their answer to the Cardinal of Guise, by all the Lutheran Churches, by all the world, says Erasmus, only now of late some have excepted themselves. But the Church of Eng-

Taylor. land chooses to follow the reason and piety of the thing itself, the example of the primitive Church, and the consenting voice of Christendom."—*Worthy Communicant*, chap. vii. sect. 1—10, vol. viii. 224, 225. Eden's ed.

"Have mercy upon us, O heavenly Father, according to Thy glorious mercies and promises; send Thy Holy Ghost upon our hearts, and let Him also descend upon these gifts, that by His good, His holy, His glorious presence, He may sanctify and enlighten our hearts, and He may bless and sanctify these gifts,

"That this bread may become the Holy Body of Christ. Amen.

"And this chalice may become the life-giving Blood of Christ. Amen."—*Office for Holy Communion.* Heber's ed., 1839, vol. xv. p. 301.

"I shall instance but once more, but it is in the most solemn, sacred, and divinest mystery in our religion, that in which the clergy in their appointed ministry do, διακονοῦντες μεσιτεύειν, stand between God and the people, and do fulfil a special and incomprehensible ministry, which the angels themselves do look into with admiration, to which, if people come without fear, they cannot come without sin; and this, of so sacred and reserved mysteriousness, that but few have dared to offer at with unconsecrated hands; some few have. But the Eucharist is the fulness of all the mysteriousness of our religion, and the clergy when they officiate here are most truly, in the phrase of St. Paul, 'dispensatores mysteriorum Dei,' dispensers of the great mystery of the kingdom. For, to use the words of St. Cyprian, 'Jesus Christ is our High Priest, and Himself became our Sacrifice, which He finished upon the cross,' &c., 452.

" . . . Now what Christ does always in a proper and most glorious manner, the ministers of the Gospel also do in theirs, commemorating the sacrifice upon the cross, 'giving thanks' and celebrating a perpetual Eucharist for it, and by declaring the death of Christ, and praying to God in the virtue of it, for all the members of the Church, and all persons capable; it is 'in genere orationis,' a Sacrifice and an instrument of propitiation, as all holy prayers are in their several proportions. . . .

"And certainly he could on no pretence have challenged the appellative of Christian, who had dared either himself to invade the holy rites within the cancels, or had denied the power of celebrating this dreadful mystery to belong only to sacerdotal ministrations. For either it is said to be but common bread and wine, and then, if that were true indeed, anybody may minister it, but then they that say so are blasphemous, they count the Blood of the Lord τὸ αἷμα τῆς διαθήκης (as St. Paul calls it in imitation of the words of Institution), the Blood of the Covenant or New Testament, a profane or common thing; they discern not the Lord's Body; they know not that the bread which is broken is the communication of the Lord's Body. But if it be a holy, separate, or divine and mysterious thing, who can make it (ministerially I mean), and consecrate or sublime it from common or ordinary bread, but a consecrate, separate, and sublimed person?

" . . . . And therefore the Christian ministry, having greater privileges, and being honoured with attrectation of the Body and Blood of Christ, and offices serving to a better covenant, may with greater argument be accounted excellent, honourable, and royal. . . .

"And certainly there is not a greater degree of power in the world than to remit and retain sins, and to consecrate the sacramental symbols into the mysteriousness of Christ's Body and Blood; nor a greater honour than that God in heaven should ratify what the priest does on earth, and should admit him to handle the sacrifice of the world, and to present the same which in heaven is presented by the eternal Jesus."—*Clerus Domini. The Divine Institution and Necessity of the Office Ministerial, written by the especial command of King Charles I.*, sec. 5, &c., Heber's ed. vol. xiv. p. 452—459.

"And, lastly (which contains the reason of the former, and of its holiness), the altar, or holy table, is *sedes Corporis et Sanguinis Christi, S. Chrysost. Hom. 21, in 2 Cor., et alibi*. We do believe that Christ is there, really present in the Sacrament; there is the Body and Blood of Christ, which are *verily and indeed taken and received by the faithful*, saith our Church. Now, if places became holy at the presence of an angel, as it did in Joshua's case, to whom the Captain of the Lord's Host appeared; and in Jacob's case, at Bethel, and in all the old law . . . . shall not the Christian altar be most holy, where is present the blessed Body and Blood of the Son of God?"

"Ay but, what when the Sacrament is gone? The relation is there still; and it is but a relative sanctity we speak of. It is appointed for His tabernacle. It is consecrate to that end.

"One thing I desire to warn you of, that is, that these phrases (scil. in the Fathers) of '*Adorato*

Altari,' and 'προσπίπτειν τῷ θυσιαστηρίῳ,' must be understood warily, and as they were meant; not that any Divine adoration was given to the altars either relatively, or transitively; but they are the metonymical expressions of the subject. For the adjuncts; adoratis altaribus: that is, adorato Christo presenti in altaribus, *inclinato capite ad altare*, that is, *inclinato capite ad Deum ibidem atque in sacris residentem*; we have good warrant to authorise this expression."—*Taylor's Works*, vol. v. p. 315.

"We (The Church of England) say, as they said, Christ's body is truly there, and there is a conversion of the elements into Christ's Body; for what, before the consecration, in all senses was bread, is, after consecration, in some sense, Christ's Body."—*Discourse of Transubstantiation, in Dissuasive from Popery*, vol. xi. p. 99.

{margin: Taylor.}

COSIN.

[John Cosin, born 1594; Dean of Peterborough, 1640; Bishop of Durham, 1661. One of the Commissioners at the Savoy Conference for revising the Liturgy.]

"Where is the danger and what doth he fear as long as all they that believe the Gospel own the true nature and the real and substantial Presence of the Body of Christ in the Sacrament, using that explication of St. Bernard concerning the manner, which he himself, for the too great evidence of truth, durst not but admit? And why doth he own that the manner is spiritual not carnal, and then require a carnal

{margin: The presence real and substantial.}

Cosin.

presence, as to the manner itself? As for us, we all openly profess with St. Bernard, that the Presence of the Body of Christ in the Sacrament is spiritual, and therefore true and real, and with the same Bernard and all the ancients, we deny that the Body of Christ is carnally either present or given. The thing we willingly admit, but humbly and religiously forbear to inquire the manner. . . . . We confess with the Fathers, that this manner of Presence is unaccountable and past finding out, not to be searched and pryed into by reason, but believed by faith. And if it seems impossible that the Flesh of Christ should descend and come to be our food through so great a distance, we must remember how much the power of the Holy Spirit exceeds our sense and our apprehensions, and how absurd it would be to undertake to measure His immensity by our weakness and narrow capacity, and so make our faith to conceive and believe what our reason cannot comprehend.

Our faith does not make the presence, it only apprehends it.

"Yet our faith does not cause or make that Presence, but apprehends it as most truly and really effected by the word of Christ; and the faith whereby we are said to eat the Flesh of Christ, is not that only whereby we believe that He died for our sins, (for this faith is required and supposed to precede the sacramental manducation,) but more properly that whereby we believe those words of Christ, 'This is My Body.' Which was St. Austin's meaning, when he said, 'Why dost thou prepare thy stomach and thy teeth? Believe, and thou hast eaten.' For in this mystical eating, by the wonderful power of the Holy Ghost, we do invisibly receive the substance of Christ's Body and Blood, as much as if we should eat and drink both visibly."—*Hist. of Transub.* p. 53, 54.

"All that remains is, that we should with faith and humility admire this high and sacred mystery, which our tongue cannot sufficiently explain, nor our heart conceive."—*Ibid.*

Again,—

"It is an article of the faith in the Church of Rome, that in the blessed Eucharist, the substance of the bread and wine is reduced to nothing, and that in its place succeeds the Body and Blood of Christ. The Protestants are much of another mind, and yet none of them denies altogether but that there is a conversion of the bread into the Body, and consequently the wine into the Blood of Christ; for they know and acknowledge that in the sacrament, by virtue of the words, and blessing of Christ, the condition, use, and offices of the bread is wholly changed, that is, of common and ordinary, it becomes mystical and sacramental food, whereby, as they affirm and believe, the true body of Christ is not only shadowed and figured, but also given indeed, and by worthy communicants truly received."—*Ibid.*

Again,—

"We confess the necessity of a supernatural and heavenly change, and that the signs cannot become Sacraments but by the infinite power of God, whose proper right it is to institute Sacraments in His Church, being able alone to endue them with virtue and efficacy. In truth, Protestants freely grant, that the wine is changed into the Blood of Christ, and firmly, as I have oft said, believe it, but every change is not transubstantiation."—*Ibid.*

THORNDIKE.

[Herbert Thorndike, Fellow of Trinity College, Cambridge, 1642; Master of Sidney, 1643; ejected by the Parliament. Prebendary of Westminster after the Restoration, one of the Commissioners at the Savoy Conference; died, 1672.]

That the Body and Blood of Christ is nevertheless present in the Sacrament, when it is received, not by the receiving of it. The words of Consecration imply as much.

"But shall this evidence of the nature and substance of Bread and Wine remaining in the Sacrament of the Eucharist, either deface or efface the evidence which the same Scriptures yield us of the truth of Christ's Body and Blood brought forth and made to be in the Sacrament of the Eucharist, by making it to be that Sacrament? Surely we must not suffer such a conceit to possess us, unless we will offer the same violence to the manifest and express words of the Scripture.

"For of necessity when our Lord saith, 'This *is* my Body,' 'This *is* my Blood,' either we must make 'is' to stand for 'signifieth,' and 'This is my Body,' 'This is my Blood,' to be no more than 'This is a sign of my Body and Blood,' or else the word '*is*' will enforce the elements to be called the Body and Blood of Christ, at that time and for that time when They are not yet received."

The elements not made the Body and Blood of Christ by the receiving of them with living faith.

"They who maintain that 'This my Body and my Blood' signifies no more but 'This is a sign of my Body and Blood,' . . . how can they ground the true and real participation of the Body and Blood of Christ in and by the Sacrament of the Eucharist

i. e. if they allow no more.

upon Scripture,[a] allowing no more than the *signification* of the Body and Blood of Christ to be declared in those words of Scripture. 'For that a man receives the Body and Blood of Christ spiritually, through faith, in receiving the Sacrament of the Eucharist, is no more than he does in not receiving the Sacrament of the Eucharist, if, by the act of a living faith we do eat the Flesh of Christ and drink His Blood, as understanding themselves aright, all Christians must needs do.'" . . .

Thorndike.

" And what a gross thing it were to say, that our Saviour took such care to leave His Church, by the act of His last will, a legacy, which imports no more than that which they might at all times bestow upon themselves." . . . . . .

" But if I allow them that make it more than such a sign to have departed from a pestilent conceit, and utterly destructive to Christianity, I cannot allow them to speak things consequent to their own position when they will not have these words to signify that the elements are the Body and Blood of Christ *when they are received*, but *become so upon being received with living faith;* which will allow no more of the Body and Blood of Christ to be in the Sacrament than out of it. For the act of living faith importeth the eating and drinking of the Flesh and Blood of Christ, no less without the Sacrament than in it. . . If 'This is my Body,' 'This is my Blood,' signifies no more than 'This is the sign of my Body and Blood,' then is the Sacrament of the Eucharist a mere sign of the Body and Blood of Christ, without any promise of spiritual grace; seeing that, being now a Sacrament, by being become a Sacrament, it is become no more than *a sign* of the Body and Blood of Christ, which, though a living faith spiritually eateth and drinketh when it receives the Sacrament, yet it should have done no less without receiving the same."—*Laws of Church*, Book iii. Ch. ii. ss. 9, 10, 1st Edit. 1659. Oxford Edit. p. 11—13.

Thorndike.

The same subject; also the eating and drinking of Christ spiritually by faith presupposes the Flesh and Blood of Christ to be previously in the elements by Consecration.

"As the eating and drinking of Christ's Flesh spiritually by faith presupposes the Flesh of Christ crucified and His Blood poured forth, so must the eating of It in the Sacrament presuppose the being of It in the Sacrament, to wit, by the being and becoming of It a Sacrament; unless a man can spiritually eat the Flesh and Blood of Christ in and by the Sacrament, which is not in the Sacrament when he eats and drinks it, but by his eating and drinking of it comes to be there."

"But if the Flesh and Blood of Christ be not there by virtue of the consecration of the elements into the Sacrament, then cannot the Flesh of Christ and His Blood be said to be eaten and drunk in the Sacrament, which are not in the Sacrament by being a Sacrament, but in him that eats and drinks it. For that which he finds to eat and drink in the Sacrament cannot be said to be in the Sacrament, because it is in him that spiritually eats and drinks it by faith. Either, therefore, the Flesh and Blood of Christ cannot be eaten and drunk in the Eucharist, or It is necessarily in the Sacrament *when* It is eat and drunk in it; in which if It were not, It could not be eaten and drunk in it."—*Ibid.* s. 12, p. 16.

The Eucharist the sacrifice of Christ upon the Cross. The eating of this sacrifice necessarily requireth the same presence of Christ (in the elements) in re præsenti.

[After quoting the words of St. Paul, 1 Cor. x. 16, 18, 21. He says (s. 14):—]

"These words manifestly suppose the Eucharist to be the communion of the Sacrifice of Christ upon the cross." . . . .

[He proceeds (s. 19):—]

"If, therefore, the eating of the Sacrifice of the Cross in the Sacrament, mean no more but the signifying and figuring of that eating of the Sacrifice of the

Cross which is done by a lively faith (that is by every *Thorndike.* one that considers the death of Christ with that faith, which, supposing all that the Gospel says of it to be true, resolves faithfully to profess Christianity), the question is, Why the sacrament of the Eucharist was instituted by God, why are those elements, and to what purpose? Seeing without God's appointment men could have done it of themselves to the same effect. But if it be manifest that by the Sacrament of the Eucharist, God pretends to tender us the communion of the Sacrifice of Christ upon the cross, then there is *another* presence of the Body and Blood of our Lord in the Sacrament, *beside* that spiritual presence in the soul which that living faith effecteth without the Sacrament as well as in the receiving of it."

" Which kind of presence, you may if you please, call the *representation* of the sacrifice of Christ; so as you understand the word 'representation' to signify not the figuring or resembling of that which is only signified, but, as it signifies in the Roman laws, when a man is said, '*representare* '*pecuniam*,' who pays ready money; deriving the signification of it *a re presenti* not from the preposition *re;* which will import, not the presenting of that again to a man's senses which is once past, but the tendering of that to a man's possession which is tendered him on the place."

[The note in the Oxford edition, p. 20, refers to a quotation from the Fathers in Bramhall's Answer to La Millitiere Works, vol. i. p. 10, note[r].]

" That this is the intent of the Sacrament of the Eucharist, one peremptory argument remains in the

Thorndike.

words of St. Paul, when he says, 'Whoso eateth this bread and drinketh this cup of the Lord unworthily, is guilty of the Body and Blood of Christ.'" 1 Cor. xi. 27. "For neither can it be said that the Apostle by way of hyperbole, calls the slighting of God's ordinance which he Had appointed to signify Christ's death, the crucifying of our Lord again, because it is manifest, that his menace is grounded upon a particular consideration of the nature of the crime, not upon that which is seen in every sin." . . . For when it follows (s. 29), "'He that eateth and drinketh unworthily, eateth and drinketh damnation to himself, *not discerning the Lord's Body;*' *unless a man discern the Lord's Body where it is not, of necessity it must there be, where it is 'discerned' to be,* not made to be there by being discerned to be there."—*Ibid.* ss. 14, 19, 20, 21; pp. 17, 20, 21.

As the properties of the Divine nature are attributed to the Manhood of our Lord, and are there by supernatural conjunction, so are the Body and Blood of Christ in the elements from consecration to receiving by supernatural conjunction and union.

"When, therefore, the properties of the Divine nature are attributed to the Manhood of our Lord (supposing, as all good Christians do, that neither natures nor properties are confounded), what can we say but this, that by such attributions as these in the language of His prophets the Apostles, God would have us understand a supernatural conjunction and union of two natures in one person in our Lord? And what shall we then say when the Name of Christ's Body and Blood is attributed to the Bread and Wine of the Eucharist, but that God would have *us understand a supernatural conjunction and union between the Body and Blood of Christ and the said Bread and Wine,* whereby they become as truly the instrument of conveying God's Spirit to them who receive as they ought, as the same Spirit was always in His natural Flesh and Blood. For it matters not that the union of the two Natures is indissoluble, that of Christ's Body and Blood only to the use of the elements (that is, properly speaking, from the consecration to the receiving), the reason of both unions being the same, that makes both supernatural ; to wit, the will of God passed upon both and understood by the Scriptures to be passed upon both though to several effects and purposes."—*Ibid.* s. 25. p. 25.

^{Thorndike.}

"He calleth His words 'spirit' and 'life,' because they are the means to bring into the communion of His Spirit, wherein spiritual and everlasting life consisteth. . . . . Those who upon faithful consideration of His cross faithfully resolve to undertake it, do by the Spirit eat His Flesh and drink His Blood. Therefore when in correspondence hereunto He pretends to institute the Sacrament of the Eucharist, that they who eat His Flesh and drink His Blood in that Sacrament may eat and drink the same spiritually (as unless they crucify Him again they cannot choose but do) it behoves indeed that *He procure the Flesh and Blood to be there by the operation of that Spirit* which framed them for an habitation to itself in the womb of the Blessed Virgin, that so the receiving of His Flesh and Blood may be the means of conveying His Spirit."—*Ibid.* s. xxxii. p. 32.

"If these things be true, it will be requisite that we acknowledge a change to be wrought in the elements by the consecration of them into the Sacrament. For how should they come to be *that which they were not* before, to wit, *the Body and Blood of Christ*, without any change ? And in regard of this

^{Change wrought in the elements by the consecration of them, they become supernaturally that which they were not before, the Body and Blood of}

Christ. The Holy Ghost makes the elements the Body and Blood of Christ dwelling in them in true being and presence, the substance of the sign still remaining, and they are the instruments of conveying His Spirit to us.

change the elements are no more called by the name of their nature or kind after the consecration, but by the name of that *which they are become*. Not as if the substance thereof were abolished, but *because it remains no more considerable to Christians;* who do not, nor are to look upon, this Sacrament with any account of what it may be to the nourishment of their bodies by the nature of the elements, but what it may be to the nourishment of their souls by the Spirit of God assisting in and with His Flesh mystically present in it. But this change, *consisting in the assistance of the Holy Ghost, which makes the elements in which it dwells the Body and Blood of Christ*, it is not necessary that we acknowledge the bodily substance of them to be any way abolished."—*Ibid.* Ch. iii. s. 1, p. 34.

"The sacramental presence of Christ's Body and Blood cannot properly be maintained, unless, acknowledging the true being and presence of the thing signified, we acknowledge the sign to remain."—*Ib.* s. 2.

The sacramental presence of Christ's Body in the Eucharistic elements (which comes to pass by the Spirit dwelling in them as in His natural Body, and so making them His Body and Blood) depends not on the living faith of him that receives, but upon their consecration by virtue of the true profession of Christianity in the Church that consecrates.

"That which I have already said is, I suppose, enough to evidence the mystical and spiritual presence of the Flesh and Blood of Christ in the elements as the Sacrament of The Same, before any man can suppose that spiritual presence of them to the soul which the eating and drinking Christ's Flesh and Blood spiritually by living faith importeth. . . .

"But then I say that *it is the visible profession of true Christianity which makes the consecration of* the Eucharist effectual to make the Body and Blood of Christ sacramentally present in the elements of it ; but that it is the *invisible faithfulness of the heart* in making good, or in resolving to make good the said profession, which makes the receiving of it effecttual to the *spiritual* eating and drinking of Christ's Body and Blood . . . . .

"But if eating and drinking the Body and Blood of Christ in this Sacrament unworthily be the crucifying of Christ again, rendering a man 'guilty' of His Body and Blood, then is not His Body and Blood *spiritually* eaten and drunk till living faith make them *spiritually* present to the soul, which the consecration maketh sacramentally present to the body. And it is to be noted that no man can say that this Sacrament *represents* or *tenders and exhibits* unto him that receiveth the Body and Blood of Christ (as all must do that abhor the irreverence to so great an ordinance which the opinion that it is but a bare sign of Christ crucified naturally engendereth), but he must believe this; unless a man will say that that which is not present may be represented, that is to say, tendered and exhibited presently down upon the place. It is not, therefore, that living faith which he that receives the Eucharist, and is present at the consecrating of it, may or may not have that causeth the Body and Blood of Christ to be *sacramentally present* in the elements of it, but it is the profession of that common Christianity which makes men members of God's Church; in the unity whereof whenever this Sacrament is celebrated (without inquiring whether those that are assembled be of the number of those to whom the kingdom of Heaven belongs), thou hast a legal presumption even towards God that thou receivest the Flesh and Blood of Christ in and with the elements of Bread and Wine, and shalt re-

_{Thorndike.}

<small>Thorndike.</small> ceive the same spiritually for the food of thy soul, supposing that thou receivest the same with living faith. For one part of our common Christianity being this, that our Lord Christ instituted this Sacrament with a promise to make by His Spirit the elements of Bread and Wine sacramentally His Body and Blood, so that His Spirit that made them so (dwelling in them as in His natural Body), should feed them with Christ's Body and Blood that receive the Sacrament with living faith; this institution being executed, that is, the Eucharist being consecrated according to it, so sure as Christianity is true, so sure the effect follows."—*Ibid.* s. 5, pp. 36—38.

" Here, indeed, it will be requisite to take notice of that which may be objected for an inconvenience that God should grant the operation of His Spirit to make the elements sacramentally the *Body and Blood of Christ* upon the dead faith of them who *receive It* to their condemnation in the Sacrament, and therefore cannot be said to *eat* the Body and Blood of Christ (which is only the act of living faith) without that abatement which the premises have established, to wit, in the Sacrament.* But all this, if the effect of my saying be thoroughly considered, will appear to be no inconvenience. For that the *Body and Blood of Christ should* be sacramentally present in and under the elements (to be spiritually received of all that meet it with a living faith, to condemn those for crucifying Christ again *that receive It with a dead faith*), can seem any way inconsequent to the consecration thereof by virtue of the

<small>Note as to the reception by the wicked.</small> * [The passage of S. Augustine quoted in the 25th Article, in reference to the eating or participation of Christ by the wicked,

common faith of Christians, professing that which is requisite to make true Christians, whether by a living or a dead faith; rather must we seek for a reason why 'he that eateth this bread and drinketh his cup unworthily' should be 'guilty of the Body and Blood of Christ' as 'not discerning It;' unless we suppose The Same sacramentally present by virtue of that true Christianity which

Thorndike.

or those who have not a lively faith.

is as follow:—all the presumed interpolations being inserted in brackets. See supra.

"And therefore who dwelleth not in Christ, and in whom Christ dwelleth not, without doubt doth neither [spiritually] eat His Flesh nor drink His Blood [albeit carnally and visibly he press with his teeth the Sacrament of the Body and Blood of Christ] but rather doth unto judgement to himself eat and drink the Sacrament of so great a thing [because being unclean he hath presumed to come unto Christ's Sacraments; which no man taketh worthily save he that is clean, of whom it is said, Blessed are the clean in heart for they shall see God."]—*August. on S. John*, ch. vi. ver. 18.

"The Note from the Benedictine edition, subjoined by the Oxford translators is this: 'So the passage stands in the earlier printed editions; but all our MSS. have it thus:—"*Nec manducat carnem ejus nec bibit ejus sanguinem, etiamsi tantæ rei sacramentum ad judicium sibi manducet et bibat;* (doth neither eat his Flesh nor drink his Blood, although he eateth and drinketh to his own condemnation the Sacrament of so great a thing)." That is, the bracketted words [spiritualiter] [licet carnaliter et visibiliter premat dentibus Sacramentum corporis et sanguinis Christi] and [quia immundus... Deum videbunt] [spiritually.] [Albeit carnally and visibly he press with his teeth the Body and Blood of Christ] and [because being unclean .... they shall see God.], are not extant in our copies. The Louvain editors also bear witness that these words are not found in their MSS. But they appear in the Commentaries of Bede and Alcuin on St. John. *Ben. ed.* Three old MSS. in the Bodleian library all omit the words in brackets."]

Thorndike. the Church professing and celebrating the Sacrament, tendereth It for a spiritual nourishment to a living faith,—for matter of damnation to a dead faith. For if the profession of true Christianity be, as of necessity it must be, matter of condemnation to him that professeth it not truly (that is to say, who professing it doth not perform it), shall not his assisting the celebration and consecration of the Eucharist produce the effect of rendering him condemned by himself (*eating the Body and Blood of Christ* in the Sacrament, out of a profession of Christianity which spiritually he despiseth), for not fulfilling what he professeth; or that living faith which concurreth to the same as a good Christian should do to be left destitute of that grace which the tender of the Sacrament promiseth, because the faith of those who join in the same action is undiscernible? Certainly if the sacramental presence of Christ's Body and Blood, tendering the same spiritually be a blessing or a curse, according to the faith which It meets with; it can by no means seem unreasonable that it should be attributed to that profession of Christianity which makes It respectively a blessing or a curse, according to the faith of them for whom it is intended."—*Ibid.* s. 6, p. 38.

The elements Christ's Body and Blood when He delivered them, not by delivery.
"When our Lord takes the elements in His hands and blesses them, or gives God thanks over them, then breaks the Bread, and delivering them, bids His disciples take and eat them because they are His Body and Blood, is it not manifest that they are so called in regard of something which He had already done about them, when delivering them He calls them at that present time of delivering, that

which He could not call them before, His Body and Blood. *Thorndike.*

"He affirmed it to be His Body at the present when He delivered it."—Ch. iv. s. 2, 6, p. 51, 52.

"Supposing Christians to believe that they are justified by *believing* that they are justified, or predestinate in consideration only of Christ's sufferings, and that the Eucharist is instituted only for a sign to confirm this faith, though they should regularly use that form of consecration which I maintain to come by tradition from the Apostles; I would not, therefore, grant that they should either consecrate the Eucharist, or could receive the Body and Blood of Christ by it. Sacrilege they must commit in abusing God's ordinance to that intent for which He never appointed it; but Sacrament there would be none further than their own imagination."—*Ibid.* c. iv. s. 25, p. 68. *Those that believe the Eucharist to be only a sign to confirm their faith do not either consecrate the Eucharist or receive the Body of Christ.*

"It is not here to be denied that all ecclesiastical writers do with one mouth bear witness to the presence of the Body and Blood of Christ in the Eucharist, neither will any of them be found to ascribe it to *anything but the consecration*, or that to any faith but that upon which the Church professeth to proceed to the celebrating of it. And upon this account when they speak of the elements supposing the consecration to have passed upon them, they always call them by the name, not of their bodily substance, but of the Body and Blood of Christ which they have become.

Justin Martyr [Apolog. I. formerly reckoned the II. s. 65, Oper. p. 52. Ed. Ben.] 'For we take them not as common bread and drink, but as our

Thorndike. Saviour Jesus Christ being incarnate by the word of God hath both flesh and blood for our salvation, so are we taught that this food, which thanks have been given for [εὐχαριστηθεῖσαν τροφὴν ζ] by the prayer of that Word which came from Him (by the change whereof are our blood and flesh nourished) is both the Flesh and Blood of Christ incarnate,' wherein divers of the Fathers have followed him. He justifies that reason of expounding 'This is my Body, this is my Blood,' which I have drawn from the communication of the properties of the several natures in our Lord Christ incarnate. But chiefly you see the elements are made the Body and Blood of Christ by virtue of the consecration, as by the Incarnation human flesh became the Flesh and Blood of Christ. So Irenæus, lib. iv c. 34. 'As the bread that comes from the earth, receiving the invocation of God upon it is not now common bread, but the Eucharist, consisting of two things, the earthly and the heavenly; so also our bodies receiving the Eucharist are not now corruptible, having the hope of rising again.' For he had argued before, that because our flesh is nourished by the Body and Blood of Christ (which if They were not in the Eucharist they could not be), therefore they shall rise again? By virtue, therefore, of the consecration They are there, not by the faith of him that receives, according to Irenæus.

Tertullian (De Resurrect. c. viii.), "The flesh feeds on the Body and Blood of Christ that the soul may be fattened with God."

Origen (In Diversis Locis, hom. v.) is the first that advises to "say with the centurion" (when thou receivest the Eucharist), "Lord, I am not worthy that thou shouldest come under my roof," for then "the Lord comes under thy roof."

S. Cyprian, upon the Lord's Prayer, having said that Christ is our bread, makes that the daily bread which we pray for, to wit in the Eucharist; and in his book "*De Lapsis*," makes it to be invading and laying violent hands on the Body of Christ for them who had fallen away in persecution to press upon the Communion without penance afore.

Thorndike.

De Orat. Dom. Oper. pp. 146. 147.

The Council of Nicæa in Gelasius Cyzicenus, ii. 30: "Let us not basely consider the Bread and the Cup set before us, but lifting up our minds, let us conceive by faith that there lies upon that Holy Table, the Lamb of God that takes away the sin of the world, sacrificed without sacrificing by priests, and that we receive truly His precious Body and Blood."

S. Hilary (De Trin. lib. viii.) censuring the Arians who would have the Son to be one with the Father as we are, maintains that we are not only by obedience of will, but naturally, united to Christ, because, as He truly took our nature, so we truly take the Flesh of His Body in the Sacrament: our Lord having said, "My Flesh is truly meat, and My Blood truly drink," and "He that eats My Flesh and drinks My Blood, dwells in me and I in him," and much more to the same purpose; which could signify nothing did not our bodies feeding upon the elements, feed upon that which is truly the Body and Blood of Christ in the Sacrament, or mystically, not by virtue of the feeding which follows, but by virtue of the consecration which goes before. For this natural union of the Body with that which feeds it, serves S. Hilary for the argument of that unity which the Son hath with

<small>Thorndike.</small> the Father by nature, being the union of our flesh with the Flesh of Christ by virtue of our flesh united to the Word Incarnate.

S. Cyril of Jerusalem (Catech. Myst. iv. & v.) argueth that Christ having said of the Bread and of the Cup, "This is My Body, this is My Blood;" who otherwhiles changed water into wine, we are not to doubt that we receive His Body and Blood under the form of Bread and Wine, and therefore we are not to look upon them "as plain bread and wine, but the Body and Blood of Christ," He having declared it; all this by sanctification of the Holy Ghost according to the prayer of the Church.

But I will go no further in rehearsing the texts of the Fathers, which are to be found in all books of controversies concerning this, for the examination of them requires a volume on purpose. It shall be enough that they all acknowledge the elements to be *changed, translated, and turned into the substance of Christ's Body and Blood*, though as in a Sacrament, that is mystically, yet, *therefore, by virtue of the consecration, not of his faith that receives*.

On the other side that this change is to be understood with that abatement which the nature and substance of the elements requires, supposing it to remain the same as it was, I will first presume from those very authors which I have quoted."

<small>Gelasius Routh Script. Eccles. Tom. ii. p. 139. S. Hilary below. Theod. in his Dialog. and many others.</small> [He then proceeds to quote a large number of authorities from the Fathers, showing that there is no tradition of the Church for the abolition of the elements, but that the substance of them remains unchanged, and concludes thus:]

<small>It is the consecration by</small> "And upon these premises I conclude, that as it

is by no means to be denied that the elements are *really changed, translated, turned, and converted,* into the Body and Blood of Christ (so that whoso *receiveth* them with *a living faith* is spiritually nourished by the same, he that *with a dead faith* is guilty of crucifying Christ), yet is not this change destructive to the bodily substance of the elements, but cumulative of them with the spiritual grace of Christ's Body and Blood, so that the Body and Blood of Christ in the Sacrament turns to the nourishment of the body, whether the Body and Blood in the truth turn to the nourishment or damnation of the soul."—*Ibid.* c. iv. ss. 27—45, pp. 69—82.

Thorndike. virtue of the faith of the Church and nothing else that turns the elements by a cumulative grace really, substantially, and truly into the Body and Blood of Christ, so that those who receive It with a lively faith receive it to their salvation, they who receive It with a dead faith to their condemnation. But the substance of the elements remains unchanged

[These sentiments are shortly restated in his "Reformation of the Church of England," ch. xxv. xxvi., vol. v. p. 542.]

[In considering the question whether the Roman Church is guilty of idolatry in worshipping the elements, he takes occasion to speak thus:—]

"I suppose that the Body and Blood of Christ may be adored wheresoever they are, and must be adored by a good Christian, where the custom of the Church which a Christian is obliged to communicate with requires it. . . . .

"But I suppose, further, that the Body and Blood of Christ is not adored nor to be adored by Christians, neither for itself nor for any endowment residing in it, which it may have received by being personally united with the Godhead of Christ, but only in consideration of the said Godhead, to which it remains inseparably united, wheresoever it becomes. For by that means whosoever proposeth not to himself the consideration of the Body and Blood of

The Body and Blood of Christ is to be adored in the Eucharist, not for its own sake, or for any of its qualities, but because inseparably united to the Godhead.

Thorndike. Christ as it is of itself and in itself a mere creature (which he that doth not on purpose cannot do), cannot but consider It as he believes It to be, being a Christian; and considering It as It is inseparably united to the Godhead, in which and by which It subsisteth, in which, that is, the Godhead, therefore, that honour resteth, and to which it tendeth—so the Godhead of Christ is the thing that is honoured, and the reason why it is honoured, both. The Body and Blood of Christ, though It be necessarily honoured because necessarily united to that which is honoured, yet is It only the thing that is honoured, and not the reason why It is honoured, speaking of the honour proper to God alone.

"I suppose, further, that it is the duty of every Christian to honour our Lord Christ as God subsisting in human flesh, whether by professing Him such, or by praying to Him as such, or by using any bodily gesture, which by the custom of them that frequent it may serve to signify that indeed he takes Him for such, which gesture is outwardly that worship of the heart which inwardly commands it. This honour then being the duty of an affirmative precept, which, according to the received rule, ties always (though it cannot tie a man to do the duty always, because then he should do nothing else), what remains but a just occasion to make it requisite, and presently to take hold and oblige.

"And is not *the presence thereof* in the Sacrament of the Eucharist *a just occasion*, presently to express by the bodily act of adoration, that inward honour which we *always carry towards our Lord Christ as God?* Grant that there may be question whether it be a just occasion or not;" [he goes on to say] "supposing the custom of the Church to have determined it, it shall be so far from an act of idolatry, that it shall be the duty of a good Christian. . . . 'If the Church hath not determined it,' (though for some occasions it may become offensive and not due) 'yet it can never become an act of idolatry.'"

Thorndike.

[He proceeds to remark that therefore he is not obliged to dispute whether in the ancient Church Christians were exhorted and encouraged to, and really did, worship our Lord Christ in the Sacrament of the Eucharist, but adds:—]

"I do believe that it was so practised and done in the ancient Church, which I maintain from the beginning to have been the true Church of Christ, obliging all to conform to it in all things within the power of it. I know the consequence to be this, that there is no just cause why it should not be done at present but that cause which justifies the reforming some part of the Church without the whole;* which if it were taken away that it might be done again, and ought not to be of itself alone any cause of distance. For I do acknowledge the testimonies that are produced out of S. Ambrose de Spirit. Sancto, iii. 12; S. Augustine, Ps. xcviii., and Epist. cxx. cap. xxvii.; S. Chrysostom, Hom. xxiv. in 1 Cor.; Theod. Dialog. ii.; S. Gregory Nazianz. Orat. in S. Gorgoniam; S. Jerom, Epist. ad Theoph.; Origen in Diversa loca Evangel., Hom. v., where he teacheth to say at the receiving of the Sacrament, 'Lord, I

* [See *post* where he says "The maintaining transubstantiation by the Romanists was a just cause for superseding the *ceremony*."]

Thorndike. am not worthy that thou shouldst come under my roof,' which to say is to do *that which I conclude*. Nor do I need more *to conclude it*.

" And what reason can I have not to conclude it? Have I supposed the elements which are God's creatures, in which the Sacrament is celebrated, to be abolished, or anything else concerning the Flesh and Blood of Christ, or the presence thereof in the Eucharist, in giving a reason why the Church may do it, which the Church did not believe? If I have I disclaim it as soon as it may appear to me for such. Nay, I do expressly warn all opinions that they imagine not to themselves the Eucharist so mere and simple a sign of the thing signified, that *the celebration thereof should not be a competent occasion for the executing of that worship, which is always due to our Lord Christ incarnate*."

The ancient Church worshipped Christ in the Eucharist, and we are therefore bound to do so, although the decree of the Tridentive Council as to transubstantiation caused the Church of England to supersede the ceremony. [After distinguishing between worshipping Christ in the Sacrament and worshipping the Sacrament, he states] that "The Council of Trent obliging all to believe the elements to be abolished and cease to be in it being consecrated, hath been a very valuable reason, though not the only reason, to move the Church of England to supersede that *ceremony* (hardly in the minds of Christians so bred to it to be parted from it), contenting itself to enjoin the receiving of it kneeling, which he that refuseth to do seems not to acknowledge the being of a Sacrament, requiring the tender of the thing signified by it and with it."

[He afterwards calls this kneeling] "that bodily gesture which professedly signifieth the honour of God tendered to Christ spiritually present in the Eucharist."—*Ibid.* lib. iii. c. 31, ss. 1—10.

[These sentiments are shortly restated in "The Reformation of the Church of England better than that of the Council of Trent," quoting the sentence of S. Augustine, "Nemo manducat nisi prius adoraverit," adding, "But this reverence is construed to be tendered to our Lord Christ as present in the Sacrament, and that presence a just occasion of tendering the same."—Ch. xlii. s. 1, vol. v, p. 586.]

Thorndike.

L'ESTRANGE.

[Hamon L'Estrange (brother of the famous Royalist Sir Roger L'Estrange), Master of the Temple, 1659.]

"Indeed if consecration be of any import, if with God it reconcileth anything effectual towards the making those elements the Body and Blood of Christ, if in us it createth any greater reverence to those dreadful Mysteries, then certainly that consecration must needs excel all others which is made in the full congregation."—(*Alliance of Divine Offices.*)

"*The Body of our Lord, &c.*] If you take a view of the elder forms, as they stand lateral to the Common Prayer, you may perceive this constituted by the coupling and uniting of the other two, which were before unlawfully divorced: for the first form in the first book, excluding the words commemorative of Christ's Death and Passion, which those Divine Mysteries were ordered to represent, as it is the precise formula of the Mass-Book, so might it be suspected as over serviceable to the doctrine of transubstantia-

L'Estrange. tion, to which the Romanists applied it. Again, in the next book, the Commemoration being let in, and the Body and Blood of Christ shut out, that Real Presence which all sound Protestants seem to allow, might probably be implied to be denied. Excellently well done therefore was it of Queen Elizabeth's reformers, to link them both together; for between the Body and Blood of Christ in the Eucharist, and the Sacramental commemoration of His Passion, there is so inseparable a league, as *subsist* they cannot, unless they *consist*. A Sacramental verity of Christ's Body and Blood there cannot be, without the Commemoration of His Death and Passion, because Christ never promised His mysterious (yet Real) Presence, but in reference to such Commemoration: nor can there be a true Commemoration without the Body and Blood exhibited and participated; because Christ gave not those visible elements, but His Body and Blood, to make that spiritual representation."—Chap. vii. p. 209.

BISHOP BULL.

[George Bull, born 1634; Bishop of St. Davids, 1705; died 1710.]

Elements upon consecration become and are made the Body and Blood of Christ. "We are not ignorant that the ancient Fathers generally teach that the bread and wine in the Eucharist by or upon the consecration of them do become and are made the Body and Blood of Christ. But we know also, that though they do not all explain themselves in the same way, yet they do all declare their sense to be very dissonant from the doctrine of transubstantiation."—*Answer to Bossuet.*

BISHOP MORTON.

[Thomas Morton, born 1564; Dean of Gloucester, 1607; Dean of Winchester, 1609; Bishop of Chester, 1615; Lichfield, 1618; Durham, 1632; died, 1659.]

"The question is not absolutely concerning a Real Presence, which Protestants (as their [the Roman Catholics'] own Jesuits witness) do also profess . . . . . Which acknowledgment of our adversaries may serve to stay the contrary clamours and calumnious accusations, wherein they used to range Protestants with those heretics who denied that the true Body of Christ was in the Eucharist, and maintained only a figure and image of Christ's Body, seeing that our difference is not about the truth or reality of the presence, but about the true manner of the being and receiving thereof."—*Catholic Appeal*, p. 93, ed. 1610.

Protestants possess a real presence.

Some ancient heretics maintain only a figure or image of Christ.

MONTAGUE.

[Richard Montague, born 1578; Bishop of Chichester, 1628; translated to Norwich, 1638; died, 1641.]

"Our formal words are: 'This *is* my body.' 'This is my blood.' This is more than this figureth or designeth. A bare sign is but a phantasm. He gave substance and really subsisting essence, who said, 'This is my body.' 'This is my blood.'"

The Eucharist more than a figure.

MEDE.

[Joseph Mede, Fellow of Christ's College, Cambridge; died, 1638.]

"Why, therefore, the all-wise God, who knew our

Mede. weakness, hath so ordained in the mystery of this Holy Sacrament, that it is a mystical Incarnation of Christ into every one who receives it. Whence Gregory Nazianzen defines the Eucharist, κοινωνία ἐνσαρκώσεως τοῦ Θεοῦ *a Communion of the Incarnation of God*. For in that He affirms the Bread to be His Body, and the Wine to be His Blood; by receiving this Body and Blood of Christ, and so changing it into the substance of our body and into our blood by way of nourishment, the Body of Christ becomes our body, and his Blood is made our blood, and we become in a mystical manner flesh of His flesh and bone of His bone. And as in His conception of the Holy Virgin, he took upon Him the nature of man, that He might save man; so in His Holy Sacrament He takes upon Him the nature of every man in singular, that He might save every man who becomes Him in the Divine Sacrament of His Body and Blood. His real Incarnation was only in one, but his mystical Incarnation in many: and hence comes this Sacrament to be an instrument whereby Christ is conveyed unto us, his benefits applied, and so our faith confirmed."—*Disc.* xlv. p. 254, ed. 1672.

"The heinousness of this sin is aggravated in respect of the thing received: for our Apostle elsewhere saith, the unworthy receiver becomes *guilty of the Body and Blood of Christ* (1 Cor. xi. 27), that is, he is guilty of offering contumely, injury, and indignity unto Him. S. Paul, when he dissuades husbands from misusing their wives, gives this for a reason, *no man ever yet hated his own flesh* (Eph. v. 29): and may not I reason thus, let no man offer injury unto Christ, because He is flesh of our flesh? Mede. yea He is our Head, and a wound or maim given to the head is more odious and dangerous than to another part. To offer violence to a common person, is a fault; to strike a magistrate, a greater; but to wound a king, who is the Lord's anointed, is a sin in the highest degree. O what a heinous sin is it then to offer violence to, and as much as in us lies, to strike and wound the Son of God, the King of Kings, and the Lord of Glory!

"To be guilty of death and shedding of the blood of any innocent man, is a fearful sin; and this made David cry out, *Deliver me, O Lord, from blood-guiltiness.* (Psalm li. 14.) How fearful is it then *to be guilty of the Body and Blood of Christ!* Whose heart is not moved against the Jews, when he hears or reads their villanies and violence offered to our Blessed Saviour? But Chrysostom gives us Chrysostom. a good take-heed, *Take heed* (saith he) *lest thou be guilty in the like kind, by unworthy receiving of the blessed Sacrament: he that defiles the King's body, and he that tears it, offend both alike; the Jews tore it, thou defilest it.* Here are (saith the same Father) *diversa peccata, sed par contumelia;* some difference of the sin, but none of the contumely therein offered.

"Joseph and Nicodemus, their pious devotion in begging and embalming the Body of Christ, is worthily recorded and commended to all generations; Mary Magdalene, in bestowing that box of precious ointment upon His holy Head hath gained to herself endless honour, instead of her former infamy: so if we receive and handle worthily this mystical Body of Christ, our portion shall be with

<small>Mede.</small> honourable Joseph and pious Mary Magdalene; our memories shall be as theirs, blessed, and our souls as theirs, to receive unspeakable comfort: but if we come unworthily, we join with Judas and the Jews, and are guilty, as they were, of the Body and Blood of Christ."—*Disc.* xlv. p. 254, 257, 268.

ARCHBISHOP BRAMHALL.

[John Bramhall, born 1593; Bishop of Derry, 1634; Archbishop of Armagh, 1661; died, 1663.]

<small>No genuine son of the Church of England ever denied a real presence.</small> "Having viewed all your strength with a single eye, I find not one of your arguments that comes home to Transubstantiation, but only to a true Real Presence, which no genuine son of the Church of England did ever deny, no, nor your adversary himself. Christ said, 'This is My Body;' what He said we do stedfastly believe. He said not, after this or that manner, *neque con, neque sub, neque trans.* And therefore we place it among the opinions of the Schools, not among the articles of our Faith. The Holy Eucharist, which is the Sacrament of peace and unity, ought not to be made the matter of strife and contention."—*Works*, fol. ed. p. 15.

"We find no debates or disputes concerning the Presence of Christ's Body in the Sacrament, and much less concerning the manner of His Presence for the first eight hundred years.

"Yet all the time we find as different expressions among those primitive Fathers as among our modern writers at this day: some calling the Sacrament 'the Sign of Christ's Body'—'the Figure of His Body'—

'the Symbol of His Body'—'the Mystery of His Body'—'the Exemplar,' 'Type,' and 'Representation, of His Body,' some saying 'that the Elements do not recede from their first nature;' others naming it 'the true Body and Blood of Christ,'—'changed, not in shape, but in nature;' yea, doubting not to say, that in this Sacrament 'we see Christ'—'we touch Christ' —'we eat Christ'—'that we fasten our teeth in His very Flesh, and make our tongues red in His Blood.' Yet, notwithstanding, there were no questions, no quarrels, no contentions amongst them; there needed no Councils to order them, no conferences to reconcile them; because they contented themselves to believe what Christ had said, 'This is My Body,' without presuming on their own heads to determine the manner how it is His Body; neither weighing all their own words so exactly before any controversy was raised, nor expounding the sayings of other men contrary to the analogy of faith."—*Ib.* p. 16.

"So grossly is he mistaken on all sides, when he saith that Protestants (he should say the English Church, if he would speak to the purpose) have a positive belief that the Sacrament is not the Body of Christ, which were to contradict the words of Christ, 'This is My Body.' He knows better—that Protestants do not deny the thing, but the bold determination of the manner by Transubstantiation."—*Ib.* p. 226.

"Abate us Transubstantiation, and those things which are consequent of their determination of the manner of Presence, and we have no difference with them in this particular. They who are ordained Priests ought to have power to consecrate the Sacrament of the Body and Blood of Christ, that is, to make them present."—*Ib.* p. 485.

FIELD.

[Richard Field, born 1561; Dean of Gloucester, 1609; described by Wood as "a principal maintainer of Protestancy, a powerful preacher, a profound schoolman," &c.]

The presence of Christ in the Sacrament said by Cajetan to be confirmed by miracles.

"The only thing he affirmeth to have been confirmed by miracles is that Christ's Body and Blood are truly present in the Sacrament, and that they are given to be the food of our souls, and that the outward elements are changed to become the Body and Blood of Christ, which we deny not, though we dissent from the Papists touching the manner of the conversion."—*Of the Church, Five Books, Appendix, folio,* p. 771.

FORBES.

[William Forbes, born 1585; Prof. of Hebrew at Oxford; Principal of the Marischal College; Bishop of Edinburgh, 1633; died 1634.]

The Body and Blood substantially present.

"The doctrine of those Protestants and others seems most safe and true, who are of opinion, nay most firmly believe, that the Body and Blood of Christ is truly, really, and substantially present in the Eucharist, and received, but in a manner incomprehensible in respect of human reason and ineffable, known to God alone, and not revealed to us in the Scriptures, not corporal, yet neither in the mind alone, or through faith alone, but in another way, known, as was said, to God alone, and to be left to His omnipotence."—*Consid. Modest. de Euchar.* I. i. 7.

BISHOP SPARROW.

[Anthony Sparrow; Fellow and Master of Queen's; Bishop of Exeter, 1667; translated to Norwich, 1678; died, 1685. One of the Commissioners for revising the Book of Common Prayer at the Savoy Conference.]

"The Priest says, 'Lift up your hearts.' For certainly at that hour when we are to receive the most dreadful Sacrament, it is necessary to lift up our hearts to God. . . .".

"Next is the Consecration. So you shall find in Chrysostom and Cyril last cited. Which Consecration consists chiefly in rehearsing the words of our Saviour's institution, This is My Body, and This is My Blood, when the bread and wine is present upon the Communion Table. 'The Holy Sacrament of the Lord's Supper,' says S. Chrysostom, 'which the Priest now makes, is the same that Christ gave to His Apostles, &c.' Again, 'Christ is present at the Sacrament now, that first instituted it. He consecrates this also: it is not man that makes the Body and Blood of Christ by consecrating the holy elements, but Christ that was crucified for us. The words are pronounced by the mouth of the Priest, but the elements are consecrated by the power and grace of God.' 'This is, saith He, 'My Body;' by this word the bread and wine are consecrated. *[The Body and Blood of Christ truly present.]*

"When the Priest hath said at the delivery of the Sacrament, The Body of our Lord Jesus Christ which was given for thee, preserve thy body and soul unto everlasting life, the communicant is to anwer Amen; by this Amen, professing his faith of the Presence of Christ's Body and Blood in that Sacrament."—*Rationale upon the Book of Common Prayer*, p. 211, 216, 220; ed. Oxford, 1840. *[Cyril. Cat. Myst. xxiii. v. c. xxi.]*

BISHOP KEN.

[Thomas Ken. Born, 1637; Fellow of New College, 1657; Bishop of Bath and Wells; one of the Bishops sent to the Tower by James II.; refused to take the Oath of Allegiance to King William; died, 1711.]

"I believe, O crucified Lord, that the Bread which we break in the celebration of the Holy Mysteries is the communication of Thy Body, and the Cup of blessing which we bless is the communication of Thy Blood, and that Thou dost as effectually and really convey Thy Body and Blood to our souls by the Bread and Wine, as Thou didst Thy Holy Spirit by Thy breath to Thy disciples, for which all love, all glory be to Thee.

"Lord, what need I labour in vain to search out the manner of Thy mysterious Presence in the Sacrament, when my love assures me Thou art there? All the faithful who approach Thee, with prepared hearts, they well know Thou art there, they feel the virtue of divine love going out of Thee to heal their infirmities and to inflame their affections; for which all love, all glory be to Thee.

"O God Incarnate, how Thou canst give us Thy Flesh to eat and Thy Blood to drink; how Thy Flesh is meat indeed; how Thou who art in heaven, art present on the Altar, I can by no means explain; but I firmly believe it all, because Thou hast said it, and I firmly rely on Thy love and on Thy Omnipotence to make good Thy word, though the manner of doing it I cannot comprehend."—*Exposition of the Church Catechism.*

SHERLOCK.

[Richard Sherlock, D.D., a Divine of eminent piety and excellence; born, 1613. Chaplain of New College, Oxford. Rector of Winwick; died, 1689. See his Life by Bishop Wilson. He was maternal uncle to the Bishop, who was indebted to him for his first instruction.]

"The sacramental Body of Christ is the consecrated Elements of Bread and Wine in the Sacrament. This is expressly affirmed by our Lord, saying, 'This is my Body; this is my Blood.' Who then dare say (as the Fathers frequently observe) 'This is not His Body, but a figure of His Body only.'

"He discerns not this Body of our Lord who sees not with the eye of faith Christ really present *under the species of bread and wine*, though he conceive not the manner thereof . . . not curiously questioning, much less pragmatically defining the way and manner of His Presence, as being deeply mysterious and inconceivable. These old verses, expressing the faith of the wisest of our first Reformers, may satisfy every modest, humble, and sober minded good Christian in this great mystery of godliness :—

> "'It was the Lord that spake it,
> He took the bread and brake it,
> And what the Word did make it
> So I believe and take it.'"

* * * * *

And he that *receives Christ's holy Body and Blood* into his soul, not first emptied of all his sins by holy faith, and all the sacred offices of true repentance, doth with Judas betray his Master into the hand of his enemies, even those very enemies which crucified Him; for those were our sins. And therefore it is

The effects of receiving Christ's Body and Blood into an impure soul.

<small>Sherlock.</small> said of such unworthy receivers that 'they are guilty of the Body and Blood of Christ.'"—*Practical Christian,* part ii. cap. i.

"I am unworthy His precious Body should be received into my soul through an unclean mouth. . . . Vouchsafe that with a pure and clean soul I may receive Thy most precious Body and Blood."

<small>The Body and Blood veiled under the species of bread and wine.</small> "Grant, holy Jesus, that as I have now received in faith Thy precious Body and Blood *veiled under the species of bread and wine,* I may hereafter behold Thy blessed face revealed in heaven," &c.—*Ibid.* part ii. cap. x.

BISHOP LAKE.

[Arthur Lake, Fellow of Winchester, 1600; Archdeacon of Surrey, 1608; Bishop of Bath and Wells, 1616; died, 1628. An eminent preacher and a man of great learning, particularly in the Fathers.]

"What good came to the elements by Consecration? Surely much; for they are made the Body and Blood of Christ. So saith Jesus, 'This is My Body,' 'This is my Blood.' The interpretation of these words is much controverted, and it is much disputed what change of the elements the words of Christ did make, for that Christ changed the bread when He consecrated it we make no doubt. The elements of bread and wine were consecrated that they might be the Body and Blood of Christ. But how are His Body and Blood to be considered? Surely not as Christ is glorified, but as He was crucified: for it is that Body that was given (as S. Paul speaketh), was broken, and the blood is that blood which was shed."
—*Sermon on Matt.* xxvi. 26, 27, 28. Sermons, 1629.

ARCHBISHOP TILLOTSON.

[John Tillotson, born 1630; Dean of Canterbury, 1672; Dean of S. Paul's, 1689; Archbishop of Canterbury, 1691; died 1694.]

"I deny not but that the Fathers do, and that with great reason, very much magnify the wonderful mystery and efficacy of the Sacrament, and frequently speak of a great supernatural change made by the Divine benediction, which we also readily acknowledge."—*Discourse on Transubtantiation.*

<small>The change made by the Divine benediction supernatural.</small>

WHEATLY.

[Charles Wheatly, born 1686; Vicar of Brent and Furneux Pelham, 1728; died, 1742. Author of "A Rational Illustration of the Book of Common Prayer."]

(Rubric.—*The Priest shall say the prayer of consecration as followeth.**)

"This prayer is the most ancient and essential part of the whole Communion office, and there are some who believe that the Apostles themselves, after a suitable introduction, used the latter part of it, from those words, 'Who in the same night,' &c. (*Alcuin de Divin. Offic.*, c. 39), and it is certain that no liturgy in the world hath altered in that particular.

"But, besides this, there was always inserted in the primitive forms a particular petition for the descent of the Holy Ghost upon the Sacramental

---

* [It is a significant fact that the term "Prayer of CONSECRATION" was not in the first or second Liturgies of King Edward VI., but was first introduced at the last revision, 1662.]

_{Wheatly.} elements, which was also continued in the first Liturgy of King Edward VI., in very express and open terms, *Hear us, O merciful Father, we beseech thee, and with Thy Holy Spirit and word vouchsafe to bless and sanctify these Thy gifts and creatures of bread and wine, that they may be unto us the Body and Blood of Thy most dearly beloved Son Jesus Christ, who in the same night, &c.* This, upon the scruples of Bucer (whom I am sorry I have so often occasion to name) was left out at the review in the fifth of King Edward; and the following sentence, which he was pleased to allow of, inserted in its stead, viz., '*Hear us, O most merciful Father, we most humbly beseech Thee, and grant that we, receiving these thy creatures of bread and wine, according to Thy Son our Saviour Jesus Christ's holy institution, in remembrance of His death and passion, may be partakers*[*] of His*

---

[*] [The words actually recommended by Bucer, were the following:—"Hear us, O merciful Father, and bless and sanctify us with Thy word and Holy Spirit, that we may, by true faith, receive in these mysteries, from His own hand, to be the meat and drink of everlasting life, the Body and Blood of Thy Son, who, in the same night," &c. The prayer for the descent of the Holy Spirit was restored as it was in King Edward's first Book to the Scotch Prayer Book, in 1636, and to the American in 1799. It is not found in any of the Liturgies of the Western Church, except the old Gallican, but is in all those of the East. Latin writers consider it as implied; and both Greeks and Latins acknowledge the Consecration to be equally valid in each rite. The present English Communion office follows the Latin rite, and Edward's first Book differed from the Greek rite in placing the prayer for the descent of the Holy Spirit, before the words of institution. Dr. Short (Bishop of St. Asaph), observes (*History of the Church of England*, Appendix E, § 745, *n.*) that "it is difficult to understand why the invocation of the Second and Third Persons in the Trinity was left out; it has been wisely restored in the American Prayer Book."]

most blessed Body and Blood, who in the same night &c. In these words, it is true the sense of the former is still implied; and, consequently, by these the elements are now consecrated, and so changed into [in the later editions the words *changed into* are altered into *become*] the Body and Blood of our Saviour Christ."—*Wheatly on the Book of Common Prayer*, 3rd edition, 1720, folio.

PELLING.

[Edward Pelling, D.D., Cambridge; Vicar of Great St. Helen's, London, 1674; Rector of St. Martin's, Ludgate, 1678; Canon of Westminster, 1683; Rector of Petworth.]

"Though there be no grounds in the world for the opinion of transubstantiation, yet we must not conceive that Christ is not verily, really, and of a truth, in the Sacrament; He may be really present, though there be no reason to believe that He is present after a corporal manner. For two different substances and natures may be joined and go together, though they remain distinct in themselves, and in their properties; as the soul and flesh of a man are united in the same person, and as the humanity and divinity of Christ were joined together in the same Lord. Though we should suppose that pillar to have been a real cloud which went before the Israelites, yet it will not follow that God was not in it; though we should suppose those shapes to have been true bodies, wherein the Spirits of God were wont to appear to the old patriarchs, yet this doth not argue that angelical substances were not present in them; though we should suppose that to have been a real dove which lighted on our Saviour, and that to have been real fire which sat upon His Apostles, yet this will not argue but that the Holy Ghost was in both. In like manner, though we grant the elements in the Eucharist to be substantially and really bread and wine, yet it will not follow by any means that Christ is not present in the Sacrament. It is easy to conceive it possible for it to be bread still and Christ's Body too, and to be wine still and Christ's Blood too. There may be a union of these two things, though we do not suppose the nature of the one to be destroyed or turned into the nature of the other.

"And that this is not only possible, but is certainly so *de facto*, the Scripture doth strongly oblige us to believe. For, 1st, S. Paul tells us, that the administration of the Sacrament is the communion of Christ's Body and Blood (1 Cor. x. 16), which words are to be understood (*vide* S. Chrysost. in 1 Cor. x. 16), not only of that federal communion which we have thereby with Christ, but moreover of that real communication which we have of Him; so that by drinking of the wine we participate of Christ's Blood, which streamed out of His side, and which He gives us here, as well as He shed it on the Cross; and by eating of the bread we do not only partake of his Body, but also obtain thereby a close conjunction and coherence with Him whose Body it is; we are united to Him by the bread, even as our flesh is united to Christ Himself, as S. Chrysostom affirms, which doth plainly argue the real presence and communication of His Body and Blood. 2nd. Again, whereas S. Paul saith (1 Cor. xi. 27), 'Whosoever shall eat this bread and drink this cup of the Lord *Pelling.* unworthily, shall be guilty of the Body and Blood of the Lord;' he doth seem manifestly to conclude, that Christ's Body and Blood is really in the Eucharist, that all worthy communicants do indeed receive Christ's very Body and Blood by receiving the elements, and that Christ's Body and Blood are verily *Christ's Body and Blood tendered to the unworthy.* tendered and offered even to the unworthy, though *they receive them not.* For were it not thus I would gladly understand how it cometh to pass, that *unworthy receiving** brings upon a man's soul some peculiar and extraordinary guilt? If it be a special sin (as S. Paul's words argue it to be) against the Body and Blood of our Lord, it must follow that the Body and Blood of our Lord are there. For a sin is of a peculiar nature and consideration when it is acted against an object that is more peculiarly interested and concerned; so the sin against the Holy Ghost seems strictly and properly to be a malicious resisting and reproaching of the truth, in spite of those miracles which are wrought by the Holy Ghost for the confirmation of the truth. A man is then said to be peculiarly guilty of the sin against the Holy Ghost, because in the working of miracles the Holy Ghost is concerned and interested after a peculiar manner. To this purpose it is observable, that when our Saviour spoke of this sin, it was after some miracle that He had done, and by occasion of the Jews reproaching it, as if it had been done, not by the power and Spirit of God, but by Beelzebub. It was especially a sin against the Holy Ghost, because

* [Note the double sense in which the author uses the word "receive."]

Polling. in the miracle the Holy Ghost was specially concerned. Even so here unworthy receiving makes a man guilty of a sin against our Lord's Body and Blood, because His Body and Blood are peculiarly interested in the Sacrament. Evil men strike at Christ then after a most sinful sort, because His Body and Blood are present there after a singular manner; and therefore doth the sin bring an extraordinary guilt, because it is the doing despite to the very Body and Blood of Him who made Himself an offering for us.

The Catholic Church in all ages believed a real presence of Christ's Body and Blood in the Sacrament. "For these and the like reasons the Catholic Church of Christ hath in all ages believed a real presence of His Body and Blood in the Sacrament, nor do I know any one doctrine of Christianity which hath come unto us with less contradiction than this came down from the very days of the Apostles, even to the very times of Berengarius. And so true is this, that the learned know well that the ancients grounded their faith of our real union with Christ upon this principle, because His very Body and Blood are really communicated to us by our receiving the Eucharist (S. Chrysostom, in 1 Cor. x. 16; vide et Iren. et multos alios). As they believed a supernatural union between the natures in Christ, so they believed a mystical union between all the faithful and Christ; and this they concluded, because they believed a Sacramental union between Christ and those creatures of bread and wine whereby we receive Christ. S. Hilary (de Trinit. lib. viii.) calls our conjunction with Christ a natural conjunction, because as our nature was before united to His by His incarnation, so now His nature is united to ours by the

Communion. Our Church calls it the Communion of the Body and Blood of the Lord, in a marvellous incorporation (Homily of the Sacrament, Pt. 1), and S. Austin himself used the same expression (S. August. Ep. ad Iren.); and all the ancients acknowledged this real union to be wrought by means of that real Communion of our Saviour's very Body and Blood, at and by the Holy Sacrament.

"For the opening now of this great mystery I shall show these five things: 1st. That we are to distinguish between Christ's natural and His spiritual body. 2nd. What is meant by His spiritual Body. 3rd. Why is it so called. 4th. That Christ hath a spiritual Body indeed. 5th. That this spiritual Body is received by us in the Sacrament.

"1st. We are to distinguish Christ's spiritual from His natural body; not as if He had two different bodies, but because that one and the same body of His is to be considered after a different manner. Now this is S. Paul's own distinction (1 Cor. xv. 44). 'There is a natural (or animal) body and there is a spiritual body. The Apostle then treats of that exalted state our bodies shall be in after the Resurrection, how they shall be delivered from all mortality and corruption, and shall be the everlasting temples of the Divine Spirit, and shall shine with light like the stars, and shall be like angelical substances and spirits in comparison; and all this because our Saviour is risen, and gone before us into heaven, and there remains in a glorious Body, as it is called Phil. iii. 21.

"Now this Body of Christ may be considered, either in respect of its own natural substance, as it

Polling. consisteth of flesh, bones, and blood, and other constituents and perfective parts of human nature; and in this sense no man can partake of the Lord's Body. Or else it may be considered with respect to his Divinity, as that is united to it, as it is clothed with infinite Majesty, as it is replenished with the presence and energy of the Godhead, as it casteth live influences upon His Church by virtue of the Godhead dwelling in it, and filleth all things with spiritual rays and emanations of His grace. In this respect our Lord is called a quickening Spirit (1 Cor. xv. 45). The first man, Adam, was made a living soul, the last Adam was made a quickening Spirit, because He giveth life to every humble and obedient heart here below, and through His human nature dispenseth to everyone the virtues of His person; and in this respect every good Christian participates of Christ's Body, that is, of the spiritualities of His glorious Body. The ancient Christians acknowledged and insisted much upon this distinction between the natural and the spiritual Body of Christ, confessing the one to be in the Sacrament, but not the other. There is, saith Clemens Alexandrinus, a twofold Blood of our Lord: there is His fleshly Blood, whereby we were redeemed from destruction, and there is His spiritual Blood, whereby we are now anointed; and this is to drink the Blood of Jesus, to be made partakers of our Lord's incorruption (Clem. Alex. Pædag. l. 2 in initio). In like manner, Origen, showing that even in the New Testament there is a letter which killeth, if men do not understand that which is said after a spiritual manner, instanceth in that phrase of eating Christ's flesh and drinking His blood; for, saith he, if you understand this according to the sound and clink of the expression, it is a killing letter (Orig. in Lev. x. Homil.). S. Jerome also tells us, that the Blood and flesh of Christ is to be understood in a twofold sense, either for the spiritual and divine Flesh and Blood, of which our Lord said, 'My Flesh is meat indeed, and my Blood is drink indeed,' or for that Flesh and Blood which was crucified, and which was poured out by the soldier's spear (S. Hieron. Comment. in Ep. ad Ephes. cap. 1). So doth S. Austin distinguish the invisible, the intelligible, the spiritual Flesh and Blood of Christ, from that visible, that palpable Body of His, which is full of grace and of the Divine Majesty (Gratian de Consecr. dist. ii. cap. 148). This he calls strictly and properly the Body of Christ; the other he calls the truth of His Body, meaning the virtue of it; and saith, positively, that till the end of the world the Lord is in heaven above; nevertheless that the truth of the Lord is with us here below. For that Body of Christ wherein he arose, is necessarily to be in one place, but the truth (or virtue) thereof is diffused everywhere (Ib. cap. 144). S. Ambrose, speaking of that Body which is received in the Eucharist, calls it the spiritual Body of Christ, the Body of a Divine Spirit (S. Ambrose de Myster. c. 9), and this I confidently affirm of all the ancients, who have either purposely interpreted or occasionally quoted those words of Christ, in the sixth of S. John, that they all understand Him to speak of our feeding upon Him after a spiritual manner, and of spiritual food, of spiritual Flesh, of spiritual Blood, which He doth give us from heaven to eat and drink of secretly and undiscernibly, always distinguishing this spiritual Body, not

Pelling.

_{Pelling.} only from the substance of the holy Elements, but also from that natural Body of Christ, which He took of the substance of the Holy Virgin."—*Discourse on the Sacrament of the Lord's Supper*, Pt. i. 1692, ch. ix. p. 224—233.

[The writer then proceeds at considerable length with his explanation; and concludes this head with observing:—]

"At present I do only suppose (what shall be showed by-and-bye) that every faithful Christian doth derive virtues from the blessed Jesus, which do relieve, and operate upon, our souls, as those virtues did upon the bodies of such as were healed and relieved by Him in the days of His flesh. For S. Luke tells us (Luke vi. 19) that there went virtue out of Him, so that He healed them all. And when that poor woman had been healed of her bloody issue only by touching our Saviour's clothes, He Himself said that virtue had gone out of Him (Mark v. 30), which story is related by S. Luke too, who adds also, that Jesus perceived that virtue was gone out of Him (Luke viii. 46). And if such wonders were wrought by the virtues of His Body in His state of servitude and humiliation, we may well believe that He now casteth upon every member of His Church more abundant virtues and influences, since His Body now is infinitely glorious and vivific by reason that the Divinity (which was hid in Him before) abideth in it in its greatest plenitude.—*Ibid.* p. 235.

"Neither is it any impropriety of speech to say that our hearts are wrought upon by the Body of Christ, that we are partakers of His Body, that we are enlivened and comforted by His very Body, when we receive those spiritual virtues which are darted from that glorified Body of His which is in heaven."—*Ibid.* p. 239.

Pelling.

[Proceeding to his 4th division, he says,] " I proceed next to show that He hath indeed such a spiritual Body, wherewith He really quickeneth and strengtheneth every faithful Christian. For the clearing hereof we must observe our Saviour's discourse with the Jews, in the sixth chapter of S. John's Gospel, by occasion of their speaking of the miracle of the manna. He told them that He would give His followers the true Bread from heaven, that His Flesh which He would give for the life of the world, should be that heavenly Bread, that His Flesh should be meat indeed, and His Blood drink indeed, and that it was necessary for every one who hoped for life to eat this Flesh and to drink that Blood of His. To conceive (as the Socinians and some other modern writers do) that by His Flesh He meant His doctrine only, and that by eating His Flesh and drinking His Blood is meant the believing of His doctrine and no more, to me seems a forced, a foreign, and very weak notion, and an inexcusable act of singularity; for all the Fathers of the Greek and Latin Churches do with one mouth interpret our Saviour's discourse of that spiritual communication of His Flesh and Blood, wherewith every good Christian is blest. Now that our Saviour might make this credible and easy to His auditors (that His Flesh and Blood should be meat and drink to the souls of His disciples), He opens the matter to them these two ways: 1st. By intimating to them that He was to ascend up in His Body into heaven (verse 62). 'What if ye shall see the Son of Man ascend up where He was before?'

<small>Pelling.</small>

'For this reason,' saith Athanasius, 'He put them in mind of His ascension into heaven, that He might draw off their minds from gross and carnal apprehensions, and that they might thenceforth know that the Flesh He spake of was to be food from above, heavenly and spiritual nourishment that He was to give them.' (Tom. i. p. 979, Edit. Par.) And this was no more impossible for Him to do than it was impossible for Him to fly through the air. He could as easily make His Body spiritual and vital as He could make an heavenly of an earthly substance, especially since He was God, which He put them in mind of by telling them that He was in heaven before.—*Ibid.* p. 242.

* * * * * "S. Austin says plainly, 'In respect of that Body which was assumed by the Word, which was born of the Virgin, which was apprehended by the Jews, which was nailed to the tree, which was taken down from the Cross, and was wrapped up and laid in the sepulchre, in respect of that Body we have Him not with us; but in respect of His majesty, in respect of His providence, in respect of His ineffable and invincible grace, that promise of His is fulfilled: Lo I am with you always, even unto the end of the world' (S. Aug. Tractat. 50 in Johan.). And speaking of the Eucharist, he doth distinguish between the Sacrament itself and the virtue of the Sacrament, calling that the grace of Christ which is not consumed with our teeth, and the participation of the Spirit (Ib. Tractat. 26, 27, in Johan.). This is that which S. Austin elsewhere calls the intelligible, the invisible, the spiritual Body of Christ; that which Irenæus calls the heavenly

<small>S. Augustine's distinction between the Sacrament and the virtue of the Sacrament.</small>

thing; that which Clement and Jerome call the spiritual Flesh and Blood of the Lord; that which pseudo Cyprian calls the Divine Virtue, the Divine Essence, the Divine Majesty, the participation of the Spirit, the drink which flows and streams from that spiritual Rock, Christ Jesus; that which S. Ambrose calls the spiritual aliment, and the Body of a Divine Spirit; that which others call the Lord's Immortality, His Divine Body, the truth of His Body, the nutriment of the inward man, the vital fulment of the incarnate Deity. And divers other expressions we meet with in old authors, signifying the wonderful virtues of Christ's glorified humanity, whereof every faithful soul is made partaker. S. Isidore Pelusiot conceived that the roasting of the paschal lamb with fire did typically signify that Christ, the true Passover, was to unite the fire of the Divine essence to His Flesh, to be eaten of us (Ep. 219, l. i.). That is his expression, and it shows his opinion, that we receive the virtue of His Divine through His human nature. Among modern foreign [?] writers none seems to me to have explained this thing better than the moderate and judicious author of the 'Diallacticon Eucharistiæ,' a book written about 130 years ago, to compose all the controversies about the Sacrament; and he, too, goes altogether this way, showing that that Body of Christ which is present with us is His spiritual Body, and that we communicate thereof by deriving efficacy, power, and vital virtue, from the Body of the Lord. And this account I am the better pleased and satisfied with, because it was a notion that was entertained and really asserted by a very learned doctor of our own Church, with whose

<small>Pelling.</small>

words I shall conclude this consideration : 'We must not collect,' saith he, 'that Christ's Body, because comprehended within the heavens, can exercise no real operation upon our bodies or souls here on earth ; or that the live influence of His glorified human nature may not be diffused through the world, as He shall be pleased to dispense it : no, we must not take upon us to limit or bound the efficacy of Christ's Body upon the bodies or souls which He hath taken into His protection : there are influences of life which His human nature doth distil from His heavenly throne. And the Sacramental bread is called His Body, and the Sacramental wine His Blood, as for other reasons, so especially for this, because the virtue and influence of His most bloody sacrifice is most plentifully and most effectually distilled from heaven unto the worthy receivers :' and many more things he saith to the same effect (Dr. Jackson, vol. iii. p. 325, et seq.).''

"By this account we may easily understand the meaning of the sixth chapter of S. John, which hath so puzzled many learned interpreters ; and we may fairly give the reason of the sentence of our Lord's : 'Except ye eat the Flesh of the Son of Man and drink His Blood ye have no life in you.' For the principle of life comes from our Lord's glorified humanity ; and unless we receive into our souls the vital virtue which distilleth from it, we can be in no other than a dead condition."

<small>The sacramental distinct from the spiritual reception.</small>

"I do not mean that 'tis impossible to have life without receiving the Sacrament ; no, there is that which divines call a Sacramental and spiritual receiving of Christ, and a spiritual receiving only

When men eat and drink after a right manner, they receive both the Sacrament and also the thing or virtue of the Sacrament; but yet men may derive, and by faith do derive, virtue from Christ without the Sacrament, if they do not abstain through negligence, or the love of sin, and the like. The grace of God is not tied to Sacraments so, but that God may dispense it as He pleaseth; nor are we to conceive that the blessed Body of Christ doth quicken none but at the Communion."—*Ibid.* pp. 247—251.

Pelling.

The res and the virtus Sacramenti here confounded.

BISHOP BURNET.

[Gilbert Burnet, Bishop of Salisbury; born, 1643, died, 1715. Author of "The History of the Reformation;" "A History of His Own Times;" "An Exposition of the 39 Articles," &c. &c.]

"It is not to be denied, but that very early both Justin Martyr and Irenæus thought, that there was such a sanctification of the elements, that there was a divine virtue in them; and in those very passages which we have urged from the arguings of the Fathers against the Eutychians, though they do plainly prove that they believed that the substance of bread and wine did still remain, yet they do suppose an union with the elements to the body of Christ, like that of the human nature being united to the divine. Here a foundation was laid for all the superstructure that was afterwards raised upon it. For though the liturgies and public offices continued long in the first simplicity, yet the Fathers, who did very much study eloquence, chiefly the Greek Fathers, carried this matter very far in their sermons and homilies. They did only apprehend the profanation of the Sacrament from the

Burnet. unworthiness of those who came to it, and being much set on the begetting a due reverence for so holy an action, and a seriousness in the performance of it, they urged all the topics that sublime figures or warm expressions could help them with."—*Art.* xxviii. p. 334. 1700. fol.

" . . . We judge that speculative opinions may be borne with, when they neither fall upon the fundamentals of Christianity, to give us false ideas of the essential parts of our religion, nor affect our practice, and chiefly when the worship of God is maintained in its purity, for which we see God has expressed so particular a concern, giving it the word which, of all others, raises in us the most sensible and strongest ideas, calling it jealousy; that we reckon we ought to watch over this with much caution. We can very well bear with some opinions that we think ill-grounded, as long as they are only matters of opinion, and have no influence neither upon men's morals, nor their worship. We still hold communion with bodies of men, that, as we judge, think wrong, but yet do both live well, and maintain the purity of the worship of God. We know the great design of religion is to govern men's lives, and to give them right ideas of God, and of the ways of worshipping Him; all opinions which *Neither transubstantiation nor consubstantiation ought to dissolve the communion of Churches.* do not break in upon these, are things in which great forbearance is to be used. Large allowances are to be made for men's notions in all other things; and therefore we think that neither consubstantiation nor transubstantiation, how ill-grounded soever we take both to be, ought to dissolve the union and communion of Churches; but it is quite another thing, *To pay divine honour to bread and wine is plain idolatry.* if under either of these opinions an adoration of the elements is taught and practised. This, we believe is plain idolatry, where an insensible piece of matter such as bread and wine, has Divine honours paid it."—*Ibid.* p. 340.

"The practice of reserving or sending about the elements began very early; the state of things at first made it almost unavoidable. When there were yet but a few converted to Christianity, and when there were but few priests to serve them, they neither could nor durst meet altogether, especially in the times of persecution. So some parts of the elements were sent to the absent, to those in prison, and particularly to the sick, as a symbol of their being parts of the body and that they were in the peace and communion of the Church. The bread was sent with the wine, and it was sent about by any person whatsoever, sometimes by boys, as appears from the famous story of Serapion in the third century . . . We can bear with the practice of the Greek Church of reserving and sending about the Eucharist,* when there is no idolatry joined with it."—*Ibid.* p. 341, 2.

"Ratramnus was commanded by Charles the Bald, then emperor, to write upon that subject, which he, in the beginning of his book, promises to do, not trusting to his own sense, but following the steps of the holy Fathers. He tells us that there were dif-

* [Burnet's opinion here may appear to some, inconsistent with the 28th article, wherein it is asserted that the Sacrament was not "reserved, carried about," &c.; but the article only says that it was not "by *Christ's ordinance* reserved," &c. It was not so done *ex precepto*, and is therefore but an act of discipline which may be altered according to circumstances by the Church's authority. See Articles xx. and xxxiv. The Sacrament is reserved for the sick in the present Church in Scotland. The Greeks reserve for the sick, but do not carry about the Sacrament in procession.]

Burnet

ferent opinions about it; some believing that the Body of Christ was there without a figure; others saying that it was there in a figure or mystery; upon which he apprehended that a great schism must follow. His book is very short, and very plain; he asserts our doctrine as expressly as we ourselves can do; he delivers it in the same words, and proves it by many of the same arguments and authorities that we bring.

"Raban and Ratramnus were without dispute reckoned among the first men of that age."—*Art. Ibid.* p. 337.

[The work of Ratramnus (or Bertram) is of peculiar importance, as it was by reading it that Ridley's opinions were formed (see supra, p. 18, 19). It is supposed to be the origin of Ælfric's Saxon Homily (see Part ii), several of the expressions in both being identical. The following are extracts:—

"'Paulo antequam pateretur, panis substantiam et vini creaturam convertere potuit in proprium corpus, quod passurum erat, et in suum sanguinem qui post fundendus exstabat.'—Sec. 28.

"'Intelligetis vere per mysterium panem et vinum in corporis et sanguinis mei conversa substantiam a credentibus sumenda.'—Sec. 30.

"'Ille panis qui per sacerdotis ministerium Christi corpus conficitur.'—Sec. 9.

"At quia confitentur et Corpus et Sanguinem Christi esse, nec hoc esse potuisse nisi facta in melius commutatione, neque ista commutatio corporaliter sed spiritualiter facta sit, necesse est ut jam figurate facta esse dicatur; quoniam sub velamento corporei panis, corporeique vini, spirituale corpus Christi, spiritualisque sanguis existit . . . . Secundum namque quod utrumque corporaliter contingitur, species sunt creaturæ corporeæ; secundum potentiam vero, quod spiritualiter factæ sunt, mysteria sunt corporis et sanguinis Christi.—Sec. 16, p. 24.

Ex his omnibus, quæ sunt hactenus dicta, monstratum est, quod corpus et sanguis Christi, quæ fidelium ore in ecclesia percipiuntur, figuræ sunt secundum speciem visibilem : At vero secundum invisibilem substantiam, *i. e.* divini potentiam Verbi, vere corpus et sanguis Christi existunt. Unde secundum visibilem creaturam corpus pascunt, juxta vero potentioris virtutem substantiæ, Fidelium mentes et pascunt et sanctificant.—Sec. 49. Lond. 1688.*]

_{Burnet.}

---

* [Dr. Hampden also (Bampton Lectures) observes: "It is a real and true presence that he, Ratramn, asserts; the virtue of Christ acting in the way of efficacious assistance to the receiver of the Sacrament. The Church of England doctrine of the Sacraments, it is well known, is founded on the views given by this Author."—P. 320. And p. 329, Lect. vii. "Both parties affirm that Christ is really and truly present in the Eucharist; both affirm that a change is worked on the bread and wine by consecration, so that they are verily and indeed the Body and Blood of Christ. But on one side it is denied that this reality and truth is to be sought in the bread and wine; or that the change is a physical one, though *real* as to efficacy or virtue. On the other side it is contended that this reality and truth of the Divine presence must be in the consecrated elements themselves, or otherwise they are mere signs without any latent virtue, that in this case the Sacraments of the new law would be inferior to those of the old law. For the latter, it was admitted, were shadows of Christ—they contained Christ in the way of anticipation:—whereas Christ's church would thus be reduced to empty signs."—P. 254.

But there is no need of a physical change to effect this.

The following additional passages from Ratramn are cited in Dr. Hampden's *Bampton Lectures*, p. 524:—

" At ille panis qui per sacerdotis ministerium Christi corpus conficitur, aliud exterius humanis sensibus ostendit, et aliud

NELSON.

[Robert Nelson, Esq., born 1656. One of the Founders of The Christian Knowledge Society; author of "The Companion to the Festivals and Fasts," (First ed. 1703), &c. Died 1715.]

"Q. In what manner was the consecration of the elements of bread and wine performed in the primitive Church?"

interius fidelium mentibus clamat. Exterius quidem panis, quod ante fuerat, forma prætenditur, color ostenditur, sapor accipitur: ast interius longe aliud multo pretiosius, multoque excellentius, intimatur; quia cœleste, quia divinum, id est, Christi corpus, ostenditur; quod non sensibus carnis, sed animi fidelis contuitu, vel aspicitur, vel accipitur, vel comeditur. Vinum quoque quod sacerdotali consecratione Christi sanguinis efficitur sacramentum, aliud superficie tenus ostendit, aliud interius ostendit. Quid enim aliud in superficie quam substantia vini conspicitur. Gusta, vinum sapit: odora, vinum redolet: inspice, vini color intuetur. At interius si consideres, jam non liquor vini, sed liquor sanguinis Christi, credentium mentibus, et sapit dum gustatur, et agnoscitur dum conspicitur, et probatur dum odoratur. Hæc ita esse, dum nemo potest abnegare, claret quia panis ille vinumque figurate Christi corpus et sanguis existit. Non enim secundum quod videtur, vel carnis species in illo pane cognoscitur, vel in illo vino cruoris unda monstratur, cum tamen, post mysticam consecrationem, nec panis jam dicitur, nec vinum, sed Christi corpus et sanguis.—Sec. 9, 10.

"Si ergo nihil hic est permutatum, non est aliud quam ante fuit. Est autem aliud, quoniam panis corpus, et vinum sanguis Christi, facta sunt . . . . Et si nihil permutationis pertulerunt, nihil aliud existunt, quam quod prius fuere . . . . Corporaliter namque nihil in eis cernitur esse permutatum. . . . Hinc etiam et sacramenta vocitantur, quia tegumenta corporalium rerum, virtus divina secretius salutem accipientium fideliter dispensat . . . At nunc sanguis Christi quem credentes ebibunt, et corpus quod comedunt, aliud sunt in specie, et aliud in significatione: aliud quod pascunt corpus esca corporea, et aliud quod saginant mentes æternæ vitæ substantia . . . Exterius igitur quod apparet, non est ipsa res, sed imago rei; mente vero quod sentitur et intelligitur, veritas rei.—*Ibid.* Sec. 13, 14, 15, 16, 48, 69, 77."]

"A. The priest that officiated not only rehearsed the evangelical history of the institution of this Sacrament, and pronounced these words of our Saviour, 'This is my Body, This is my Blood,' but also offered up a prayer of consecration to God, beseeching Him that He would send down His Holy Spirit upon the bread and wine presented to Him upon the altar, and that He would so sanctify them, that they might become the Body and Blood of His Son Jesus Christ, not according to the gross compages or substance, but as to the spiritual energy and virtue, of His holy Flesh and Blood, communicated to the blessed elements by the power and operation of the Holy Ghost descending upon them; whereby the Body and Blood of Christ is verily and indeed taken by the faithful in the Lord's Supper. This prayer is found in all the ancient Liturgies, and some learned men have thought that St. Paul alluded to something of this nature, when he speaks of the offering of the Gentiles being made acceptable by the sanctification of the Holy Ghost, there being no less than five liturgical words in that text, as has been observed by learned men."*

"Q. How ought we exercise our devotion on a sick bed?—A. By desiring the assistance of a spiritual guide to offer up our prayers, and to support our weakness by the most comfortable viaticum of the blessed Sacrament, &c.

"O merciful Jesu, let that immortal food which in the holy Eucharist thou vouchsafest me, instil into my weak and languishing soul new supplies of grace."
—*Companion for the Festivals and Fasts, last ed. of the Christian Knowledge Society*, 1852.

* "Iren. l. 4. c. 34, l. 5. c. 2;—Basil. de Spir. san. tom. 2. c. 27; Cyr. Hier. Cat. Myst. 5, § 5. Origen, cont. Cels. lib. 8.

BISHOP WILSON.

[Thomas Wilson, Bishop of Sodor and Man, born 1663, educated in Trinity College, Dublin, consecrated Bishop, 1698; died 1755].

"We offer unto Thee, our King and our God, this bread and this cup. We give thee thanks for these and for all Thy mercies, beseeching Thee to send down Thy Holy Spirit upon this sacrifice, that He may make this bread the Body of Thy Christ, and this cup the Blood of Thy Christ, and that all we who are partakers thereof, may thereby obtain remission of our sins, and all other benefits of His passion."—*Sacra Privata*. ("Lord's Supper; immediately after the Prayer of Consecration.") Cleaver's ed. p. 79.

"He then offered up Himself to God in the symbols of bread and wine, as a pledge of His real and natural Body which He was just going to offer to God for the sins of the world. *His Sacramental Body* was given, offered, before He suffered. It was made His Sacramental Body by His Almighty Word, none but God could do it, we therefore invoke the Holy Ghost one God with Him, to make the elements what Christ Himself made them, His Sacramental Body, it being the Spirit that quickeneth, the flesh profiteth nothing. . . . It is the Spirit, *i. e.* the Holy Ghost, sent upon them in the prayer of the priest, which conveys to us the seed of eternal life."—*Ibid. Parker's ed.* 1853, p. 107.

Rit. Græc. Grab. in Just. Apol. 1. p. 327. Church Catechism." "The merits of these three works, "The Practice of True Devotion," "The Companion for the Festivals and Fasts," and "The Great Duty of frequenting the Christian Sacrifice," seemed from the first, to have excited the admiration and gratitude of the members of the Society for Promoting Christian Knowledge, one of whose pleasing duties and valuable privileges it has ever been, to

GRABE.

[John Ernest Grabe, a learned Prussian, born 1666; left the Lutheran communion to embrace that of the English Church; came to reside in England in 1695, in order to unite himself openly to the same; afterwards took holy orders; ordained Priest in 1700, received the degree of D.D. from the University of Oxford in 1706; died in 1711. He edited "the Septuagint, and Bishop Bull's works; and, besides his published works, as (Notes to his edition of Irenæus, Justin Martyr, &c.,) he left many unpublished manuscripts which are all now in the Bodleian Library, at Oxford, with the exception of his treatise on the "Schism and Errors of the Lutherans," which has been abstracted from that Library. He had a great esteem for Edward's First Book of Common Prayer, as may be observed on reading his work, " De formâ Consecrationis Eucharistiæ."]

[Commenting on the texts, 1 Cor. xii. 27, " Ye are the Body of Christ," and vi. 15, " What, know ye not that your bodies are the members of Christ?" and ver. 19, " What, know ye not that your body is the temple of the Holy Ghost?"—Dr. Grabe says,] " As, therefore, the faithful are called the Body of Christ, and their bodies the members of Christ, because in them the Spirit and the same Divine grace resides, as in His Body, although it dwell not after the same measure; therefore, the Church has always believed that the bread and wine, after consecration, is named, and is, the Body and Blood of Christ; firmly persuaded that the Holy Ghost, and all Divine grace and virtue with which the Flesh and Blood of Christ abounds, descends not immediately into the souls of the faithful communicants

The Holy Ghost descends not immediately into the soul, but on the sacramental symbols.

distribute among their fellow-believers, such helps to the knowledge of the truth, to the steady practise of true piety, and to the increase of pure devotion." *Preface of the Society for Promoting Christian Knowledge.*]

Grabe.

Calvin.

The Consecration.

(which is the opinion of Calvin and his followers), but from Heaven, on the very Sacramental Symbols, and wholly sanctifies them, and through them, all who worthily feed on them. . . . Hence the Latin word 'consecratio,' and the Greek ἁγιασμὸς, by which, not only the separation of bread and wine to a sacred use taketh place by any minister at the sacred altar; but the very sanctification of them by the Spirit of God, at the prayer of the priest, ever was denoted."—*Notes to Irenæus*, p. 399.

RANDOLPH.

[Thomas Randolph, born, 1700; Archdeacon of Oxford, 1767; Prof. 1768; died, 1783.]

"A like instance of moderation is plainly to be seen in the XXVIIIth Article. They purposely avoided defining the manner of *His presence in the Lord's Supper*. Nay, they struck out part of an article among them, drawn up in King Edward the VIth's time, which seemed to deny all *corporal presence*, and to which therefore, the Lutherans might scruple subscribing, and contented themselves with condemning those only who held the doctrine of Transubstantiation or affirmed that the Body of Christ was eaten after a carnal manner.—*Bp. Burnet Hist. of Reform.*, vol. ii. lib. 3, 405." *Randolph's Sermons.*, vol. i. p. 496.

BISHOP WARBURTON.

[William Warburton, born 1698; Dean of Bristol, 1757; Bishop of Gloucester, 1759; died 1799. One of the most eminent scholars and divines of the age. Author of "The Divine Legation," &c.]

The words of institution, 'Hoc est corpus'

"The learned Catholic Bishop [Bossuet] saith true, that Protestants have but lamely justified the

FIGURE of 'This is my Body,' &c., by those others of 'I am the Vine,' 'I am the Door.' And his reason is solid. 'Jesus,' saith he, 'in the institution of this rite was neither propounding a parable, nor explaining an allegory.'"—*Discourse on the Lord's Supper, Works*, vol. x.

<small>Warburton. ———— meum,' not to be understood figuratively.</small>

[" The business in hand," observes Bossuet, " was the institution of a new rite, which required the use of simple terms, and that place in Scripture is yet to be discovered, where the sign hath the name of the thing signified given to it at the moment of the institution of the rite, without any leading preparation."*]

---

* [Ernesti in his *Institutes* adopts the same principle of interpretation: "Legislators in their edicts, historians in their narratives . . . . and finally the teachers of any system, when their object is simply and clearly to convey their dogmas, not touching upon them casually or for some other purpose . . . all these are in the habit of using proper diction, and of avoiding tropes, except such as from usage have acquired a *proper* sense. In such compositions, therefore, we must not admit a tropical sense, unless it can be clearly shown that such a sense has become almost proper by the usage of all writers, or at least of the particular writer under examination. . . . Therefore, as in Matt. xxviii. 19, we understand $\beta\alpha\pi\tau i\zeta\epsilon\iota\nu$ properly, though it is sometimes used tropically, so by parity of reason in Matt. xxvi. 27, 28, *To eat the Body of Christ, and to drink his Blood*, must be understood *in its proper sense, though in* John vi. *it be used tropically* . . . Thus, if we compare Matt. xxvi. 28 with Heb. ix. 20, it follows from this principle that $\tau o\hat{v}\tau\acute{o}$ $\acute{\epsilon}\sigma\tau\iota$ $\tau\grave{o}$ $\alpha\hat{\iota}\mu\alpha$ $\tau\hat{\eta}s$ $\delta\iota\alpha\theta\acute{\eta}\kappa\eta s$ is in both texts to be interpreted in a proper sense. For no one doubts but that in Hebrews the sense is proper; much more must this be the case in the antitype, Matt. xxvi. 28; nor could that expression convey any other than its proper sense to the minds of the disciples, who were accustomed to understand Christ's declarations in their proper sense."—Part I. s. ii. ch. iv. x. xii. p. 120, 122.—See also *Supra*, p. 61, *note from Wilson*.

Dr. Terrot, now Bishop of Edinburgh, observes, in his note to his translation of Ernesti's "Institutes," p. 147, that "the reader

PALMER.

[William Palmer, Rector of Whitchurch Canonicorum, Author of Horæ Liturgicæ.]

Treatise on the Church, 1838. *Second edition*, 1839, dedicated, with permission, to the Archbishops of Canterbury and Armagh.

" The injunction of the English Church [see Golden Canons], * * * most fully recognises the guidance of tradition in matters of faith . . . . The reverence of the Church of England for the tradition of the Universal Church in all matters of doctrine and discipline, is so manifest, and the consent of her theologians at all times so perfectly accordant with

may be surprised at finding the Protestant Ernesti so anxious to maintain the *proper* sense of the form of the Eucharistic Institution. But it must be remembered that he was a Lutheran, and as such bound to support the doctrine of consubstantiation, which he does by the same arguments and texts as Jahn, a Romanist, uses for the support of transubstantiation." He adds that "perhaps" the Apostles, until the day of Pentecost were too much in the habit of construing their Master's declarations in a literal sense." On this subject see Dr. Wright's observations in his translation of Seiler's Hermeneutics (Note on Part 1, ch. ii. p. 82). Ernesti's opinion that John vi. must be tropically interpreted is of less moment; as, although the Fathers in general apply this chapter to the Eucharist, in which they have been followed by many of the moderns, and although Calvin has founded his views on the Eucharist on this very chapter, yet it is not *certain*, as is the case with the former passage (Matt. xxvi.), that it does relate to the Sacrament, and many of the most eminent commentators, ancient and modern, including Roman Catholics* and Protestants, have given it a tropical interpretation, and denied its application to the Eucharistic institution. Jahn, the eminent theological professor here alluded to, observes that John vi. 29, 35, 40, 46, 47, is to be reckoned among ambiguous passages, and that it seems to be

---

* [See some of these enumerated by Jeremy Taylor in his "Real Presence."—*Heber's ed.* 1839, pp. 438, 439.]

the same sentiment . . . the Church of England has a fixed rule to guide her in the interpretation of Scripture, and a rule which is also acknowledged by all the rest of the Catholic Church."—Vol. i. p. 226. "It is certain that the Church of England, and the whole body of our eminent and learned theologians receive the doctrine of the Church Universal, and the Apostolic tradition, with great reverence and devotion."—*Ibid.* p. 252).

"There is another principle of the Church of England, which is in the highest degree calculated to preserve her in unity of faith. That principle is contained in the XXth Article, 'The CHURCH hath . . AUTHORITY IN CONTROVERSIES OF FAITH :' that is, not only have National Churches the power of defining the faith for their own members, but National Churches themselves are subject, in matters of faith, to the superior authority of the Universal Church. The opponents of the Church of England cannot deny that she really claims authority for the Church. . . ."—*Ibid.* p. 227.

"Are we accused of denying the Real Presence? Milner and Hornyhold acknowledge our perfect belief of that doctrine."—*Ibid.* p. 232.

intimated there that Jesus speaks of faith in himself, and that this faith was the life-giving bread. But because he did not more clearly instruct those who were offended, understanding his words properly, (merely saying that 'it is the spirit that quickeneth, and that the flesh profiteth nothing,' ver. 63.), and as he expressly said that his flesh which he was about to give for the life of the world was meat indeed (ver. 51), and even distinguishes the flesh from the blood, saying that the one was to be eaten and the other drunk; (ver. 63), not a few still take Christ's words properly, and the controversy can scarcely be decided. Perhaps he spoke tropically, with, however, an allusion to the Eucharist, which he was about to institute."—*Enchiridion.* p. 112.

Palmer.

"This Catholic and Apostolic Church has always avoided any attempt to determine too minutely the mode of the true Presence in the Holy Eucharist. Guided by Scripture, she establishes only those truths which Scripture reveals, and leaves the subject in that mystery, with which God for His wise purposes has invested it. Her doctrine concerning the true Presence appears to be limited to the following points:—

"Taking as her immovable foundation the words of Jesus Christ: 'This is My Body ... This is My Blood of the new Covenant;' and 'Whoso eateth My Flesh and drinketh My Blood hath eternal life;' she believes that the Body or Flesh, and the Blood of Jesus Christ, the Creator and Redeemer of the world, both God and man, united indivisibly in one Person, are verily and indeed given to, taken, eaten, and received by the faithful in the Lord's Supper, under the outward sign or form of Bread and Wine, which is, on this account, the 'partaking or communion of the Body and Blood of Christ.' She believes that the Eucharist is not the sign of an *absent* body, and that those who partake of it receive not merely the figure, or shadow, or sign of Christ's Body, but the reality itself. And as Christ's divine and human natures are inseparably united, so she believes that we receive in the Eucharist, not only the Flesh and Blood of Christ, but Christ Himself, both God and man.

"Resting on these words, 'The Bread which we break is it not the communion of the Body of Christ?' and again, 'I will not drink henceforth of this fruit of the Vine;' she holds that the nature of the Bread and Wine continues after consecration, and therefore rejects transubstantiation, or '*the* change of the substance' which supposes the nature of bread entirely to cease by consecration.

"As a necessary consequence of the preceding truths, and admonished by Christ Himself, 'It is the Spirit that quickeneth, the flesh profitteth nothing: the words that I speak unto you they are Spirit and they are life;' she holds that the Presence (and therefore the eating) of Christ's Body and Blood, though true, is altogether 'heavenly and spiritual,' of a kind which is inexplicable by any carnal or earthly experience or imagination; even as the Sonship of the Eternal Word of God, and His Incarnation, and the Procession of the Holy Spirit, are immeasurable by human understandings.

"Believing, according to the Scriptures, that Christ ascended in His natural Body into Heaven, and shall only come from thence at the end of the world; she rejects for this reason, as well as the last, any such real Presence of Christ's Body and Blood as is 'corporal' or organical, that is, according to the known and earthly mode of existence of a body.

* * * * * * *

"Such is the simple, the sublime, and, what is more, the true and scriptural doctrine of our Catholic and Apostolic Church—a doctrine which cannot be accused of heresy except from ignorance or uncharitableness. Even our adversaries are compelled sometimes by the force of truth to clear the Church of England from the imputation of disbelieving the sublime mysteries of this Holy Sacrament, and reducing it to a common spiritual exercise, in which the mind of the individual derives edification, and perhaps grace, from the contemplation and remembrance of an absent Redeemer's sufferings.

<small>Palmer.</small>

"Our doctrine leaves this subject in the sacred mystery with which God has enveloped it. It is not to be denied that the Roman doctrine of transubstantiation facilitates the mental conception of that mystery; but it has the fatal defect of being opposed to the plain language of Scripture; and if those statements are to be explained away, and reduced to merely figurative expressions, according to the doctrine of Paschasius Radbertus and his school; the Berengarians, Zuinglians, and Socinians, may with reason claim a similar privilege of arbitrarily explaining away into figures the very passages in which the doctrine of the true Presence itself is conveyed.

"The Roman doctrine of transubstantiation is entirely founded on human reasoning from the nature of bodies, and the supposed incompatibility of the scriptural statement that the Eucharist is bread and wine, literally understood, with the other expressions of Scripture. But what Bossuet has observed of the philosophical reasonings of the schools of Zurich and Geneva against the real Presence, 'que les reçevoir en matière de religion, c'est détruire non seulement le mystère de l'Eucharistie, mais tout d'un coup tous les mystères du Christianisme," is perfectly applicable to those of Romanists for their transubstantiation."—*Ibid.*, pp. 526—533.

* * * * * * *

"It is a pious, probable, and catholic opinion, that the wicked eat not the Flesh of Christ in the Eucharist, because our Lord himself said, 'He that eateth my flesh and drinketh my blood hath eternal life,' but since these words may possibly refer to a *worthy* participation of the Lord's Supper, and since many in the Church have held that the wicked do in fact receive the Body of Christ, though to their condemnation; this doctrine is taught by the Church of England as the more pious and probable opinion, not as a matter of faith necessary to be believed by all men, for this would amount to a condemnation, not only of the Roman churches, but of the Lutherans, as heretical, which has never been the doctrine of this Church."*—*Ibid.* vol. ii. p. 263.

". . . The articles comprehend not only doctrines of faith and morals, but historical and theological verities, and pious catholic and probable opinions.

"This is the sentiment of our theologians, Hall, Laud, Bramhall, Stillingfleet, Sparrow, Bull, Burnet, Nicholls, Randolph, Cleaver, &c., who understand that all the doctrines of the articles are not fundamental or necessary to salvation, or articles of faith." —*Ibid.* p. 264.

". . . . The authorised doctrine of the Church of England, during the whole of Edward VI.'s reign, was that of the Real Presence, in the strongest and most decided sense (vol. i. p. 511). It is true that there were considerable discussions and controversies concerning the mode of the Presence, between Cranmer, Ridley, Poynet, &c., on the one side, and Gardiner, Tunstall, and Smythe, on the other; and therefore, it may be concluded, that at that time the *mode* of the Presence was held undecided by the Church of England, as, in fact, she had avoided the term transubstantiation in the Necessary Doctrine, and while a change of substance was there strongly asserted, this might be understood in several senses,

* [See the note on St. Augustine's views regarding the mandu-

though I admit that transubstantiation is the more natural meaning. The Real Presence, however, was then professed by all parties. I need not speak of Gardiner and Smythe, who went into the extremes of the Romish opinions; but it was not confined to them. Dr. Oglethorpe, in his 'Submission and Profession of Faith,' A.D. 1550 (having been accused of being opposed to the Service Book, and the king's proceedings), was permitted to declare, that while he rejected the doctrine of transubstantiation, he held ' that there is a certain, and an ineffable presence of Christ's Body there, which I can neither comprehend nor express,' &c. Bishop Ridley protested, that in opposing the doctrine of the corporal presence, he did not mean 'to remove that Real Presence of Christ's Body in his Supper, duly and lawfully administered, which is founded in the Word of God, and illustrated by the commentaries of the orthodox Fathers. Bishop Poynet maintained the doctrine of the Real Presence in his book on the Eucharist in a very decided manner. Bucer and Melancthon, whom Cranmer invited to England, had always maintained the Real Presence, as even Gardiner admits.—*Cranmer's Works*, vol. iii. pp. 54, 55, 167."—*Ibid.* vol. i. p. 512.

"The declaration on kneeling at the Sacrament, contained in the ritual of 1552, and which is said to convey the doctrine of Zuinglius on the Eucharist (*Bossuet Var.* liv. vii. s. 82), cannot be considered cation by the wicked (supra, p. 57—61). Jeremy Taylor ("Real Presence," ed. 1839, p. 427,) adds the following illustrative passage from Bellarmine: "Apud Augustinum sæpissime, illud solum dici tale, et veré tale, quod habet effectum suum conjunctum; res enim ex fructu æstimatur; itaque illos dicit veré comedere corpus Christi, qui utiliter comedunt."]

as a definition of doctrine made by the Church of England, for . . the bishops and clergy were not then bound to declare their assent to everything comprised in the ritual; they were only bound to perform the rites therein contained, of which this declaration was no part. Its intention, however, was merely to prevent the worship of bread and wine in the Eucharist, which would be decidedly idolatrous; and to reject such a real presence of Christ's body as is corporal and organical; since the body of Christ in its natural mode of existence can only be in heaven" . . . . (*Ibid.* p. 513, 514.)

"Bossuet (Var. xiv. 122.) affirms that even the Declaration against transubstantiation leaves the English at liberty to believe that the body and blood of Jesus Christ are really and substantially present in the bread and wine immediately after consecration."—*Ibid.* p. 531.

"It seems plain, indeed, that during the whole reign of Edward VI. the doctrine of the Church of England was most authentically represented by the formulary of instruction formally approved by the Convocation in the reign of Henry VIII, A.D. 1543, entitled 'The Necessary Doctrine and Erudition;' a book which was most assuredly quite opposed to the Zuinglian doctrines . . . . At the end of this [first] book of Homilies, we read of 'the due receiving of Christ's Body and Blood under the form of bread and wine;' this is all very consistent with the Necessary Doctrine, but it is not Zuinglian."—*Ibid.* p. 509, 510.

[Speaking of the year 1558,] "Burnet says: 'It was proposed to have the Communion Book so contrived that it might not exclude the belief of the corporal

Palmer.

presence, for the chief design of the Queen's council was to unite the nation in one faith, and the greatest part of the nation still continued to believe such presence.' (*Burnet*, vol. ii. p. 704.) ... What the proof of this is, I have yet to learn, and Burnet himself, thirty-three years afterwards, gave an account of the matter, from which it may be suspected that he drew on his own imagination for the reason assigned in the above passage. 'The most material (difference) is the leaving out of that express declaration that was made against the corporal presence of Christ in the Sacrament, which I then thought was done in compliance with the opinion prevalent among the people of the Popish persuasion, who were strangely possessed with the belief of such a presence; but I am convinced by the letter sent to me from Zurich, that in this, great regard was likewise had to the Lutheran Churches, with whom a conjunction was much endeavoured by some.' (*Ibid.* vol. iii. p. 518.) ... They [the changes] may have been made chiefly for their own sakes, on the principle of not putting forward mere human reasonings, or anything else which might seem harsh in tone, or be in any way construed into a doubt of the real presence ... If there had been an intention to facilitate the union of those who believe the corporal presence, there would not have been any evident inconsistency with the faith of Cranmer and his companions in suffering ... If the Necessary Doctrine maintains a change of substance in the Eucharist, without affirming transubstantiation, the Article in denying transubstantiation does not condemn absolutely all change of substance in any sense,* but the

* "*E. g.* If we do not take the term substance in the scholastic sense, as distinguished from the accidents, and if the change is not

particular change called by the Romanists transubstantiation, which supposes the bread to cease to exist."—Vol. i. pp. 520—524.

"... Particular churches are liable to involuntary error without heresy, and may in some points change their opinions without heretical variation. Altogether I see not that there is any very great contradiction between these two formularies [the Necessary Doctrine, and the XXXIX. Articles] in matters of doctrine. I dispute not that several of those who composed the one differed in some points from several of those that composed the other; but their formularies are not so worded as to evince any great or irreconcilable opposition between the public and authorised faith of the Church of England in the reign of Henry VIII. and that of Queen Elizabeth."—*Ibid.* pp. 526.

REV. E. HAROLD BROWN. M.A.

[Norrisian Professor of Divinity in the University of Cambridge.]

Exposition of the Thirty-nine Articles, 2nd. ed. London, 1854.

" It is not even denied that we receive [Christ's] Body really, substantially, corporally; for though the word *corporally* seem opposed to 'spiritually,' yet not of necessity. And, as we acknowledge that it is a Body which we receive, so we cannot deny its corporal or in any sense carnal, but mystical, or spiritual, or moral. Some change of the bread and wine all orthodox Christians allow. Bishop Pearson says truly that the μεταστοιχείωσις of the sacramental elements maketh them not to cease to be of the same nature which before they were."—Creed, Art. III. The term substantial is used by Bishop Poynet, in his " Diallacticon," ... to express the true presence. The confession of Augsburg is said .. to have taught the real and " substantial " presence, which is also affirmed in the Lutheran Formula Concordiæ, pt. i. Art. vii.

Brown. presence corporally, *i. e.* after the manner of a Body." Only, when we come to explain ourselves, we say that though it be Christ's very Body we receive in the Eucharist, and though we cannot deny even the word *corporal* concerning it; yet as Christ's Body is now a spiritual Body, so we expect a spiritual presence of that Body; and we do not believe that we *naturally* and *carnally* eat that which is now no longer carnal and natural; but that we spiritually receive Christ's spiritual Body into our souls, and spiritually drink His life-giving Blood with the lips of our spirit."—*Exposition of the 39 Articles.* Art. xxviii., 2nd. ed. 1854, p. 680.

We do not eat Christ's body naturally or carnally.

"In one sense of the words we may admit that every communicant eats Christ's Body and drinks his Blood."—*Ibid.* p. 729.*

"In the former (1 Cor. xi.) we are told that 'whosoever shall eat this bread and drink this cup of the Lord unworthily, is guilty of the Body and Blood of the Lord' (ver. 27), and that 'he that eateth and drinketh unworthily, eateth and drinketh condemnation to himself, not setting apart as holy the Lord's Body' (ver. 29) . . . The unworthy communicant is 'guilty of the Body and Blood of the Lord,' which he pollutes, and he eats and drinks condemnation, because he does not set apart and treat with reverence the Lord's Body. At least candour may oblige us to admit that there is nothing in St. Paul's words thus cited which will not square with the hypothesis that every recipient equally eats the Flesh and drinks the

The unworthy communicant.

---

* [He instances the opinion of the wicked eating " the symbol which is called his Body ('corpus, *i. e.* figura corporis'), and drinking the symbol which is called his Blood." Thus Cranmer on one occasion explains " sacramentally " by " figuratively." See p. 19.]

Blood of Christ. But on the other hand, we are justified in contending that there is nothing inconsistent with our own belief, that the wicked do not eat Christ. In the former case we can see how great the profanation would be; but in the latter it is still very fearful. The feast provided for the faithful is doubtless a spiritual feast on the Lord's Body and Blood, hence the profane receiver is unquestionably 'guilty concerning Christ's Body and Blood.' And, again, as the bread and wine are the means of communicating to us the Body and Blood of Christ; so he who treats the Eucharist as part of a mere common feast (which the Corinthians did), does clearly refuse to treat with reverence, and to set apart as holy, the Body of the Lord."—*Ibid.* art. xxix. pp. 730, 731.

"The doctrine of Transubstantiation and (as it is improperly called), the *real presence*, is the established doctrine of the Roman Church. There is still, however, a room for difference of statement, and difference of thought, upon the subject. It appears to be ruled that the substance only, not the accidents, undergo a change. Now it is almost questionable whether the accidents do not comprise all the properties of matter. If so, the change may still be spiritual rather than material. . . . . . In the Eucharist, the learned and enlightened appear to acknowledge a far more spiritual change than is taught to the equally devout but more credulous multitude. For the latter all kinds of miracles have been devised, and visions wherein the Host has seemed to disappear, and the infant Saviour has been seen in its room, or where blood has flowed in streams from the consecrated wafer, impiously preserved by unbelieving communicants. But, on the other hand, by the more learned and liberal, statements have been made perpetually in acknowledgment of a spiritual rather than a carnal* presence, and such as no enlightened Protestant would cavil at or refuse."—Art. xxviii. p. 700.

"St. Bernard of Clairvaux . . . (A.D. 1115) acknowledged no feeding but a spiritual feeding. Peter Lombard, the famous master of the sentences (A.D. 1141), though speaking of the conversion of the bread and wine, declines to determine whether that conversion be formal or substantial, or of some other kind. Aquinas (A.D. 1255), spoke of Christ's Body as present, not bodily, but substantially; a distinction not easy to explain. . . . . Cuthbert Tonstal, Bishop of Durham, said that 'Before the Lateran Council it was free to every one to hold as they would concerning the manner, and that it would have been better to leave curious people to their own conjectures.' Cardinal Cajetan writes that 'The real Body of Christ is eaten in the Sacrament, yet not corporally, but spiritually. Spiritual manducation, which is made by the soul, reaches to the Flesh of Christ, which is in the Sacrament.' And Gardiner, in his controversy with Cranmer, says, 'The Catholic teaching is that the manner of Christ's presence in the Sacrament is spiritual and supernatural, not corporal, nor carnal, not natural, not sensible, not perceptible, but only spiritual, the how and manner whereof God knoweth.'—*Cranmer, Works,* vol. iii. p. 241." *Ibid.* p. 701.

* [It is evident that the impugners of the doctrine of Transubstantiation, cited in this Catena, included under that term, the notion of a *physical* Presence.]

BEAUMONT.

[Joseph Beaumont, D.D., born A.D. 1605; Fellow of Peterhouse; ejected from his Fellowship at Peterhouse, 1651; after the Restoration, twenty-nine years Regius Professor of Divinity in the University of Cambridge; Master of Jesus College, 1661; of Peterhouse, 1663; and one of King William's Commissioners, 1689; died, 1699. The first edition of "Psyche, or, Love's Mystery," displaying the intercourse between Christ and the Soul, was published in 1642, and the second, considerably enlarged by the Author, was published by his only son, the Rev. Charles Beaumont, Fellow of Peterhouse, in 1702. It is called by Southey, (Notes to Life of Wesley,) "one of the most extraordinary poems in this or any other language."]

Extract from "Psyche."

CANTO XII.

THE BANQUET.

85.

But Christ's adorable design was now
    With such a royal feast to bless the board,
As might make *spirits*—fat and heathful grow,
    And thriving nutriment to *souls* afford.
        Such nutriment as might full powér give
        Unto His guests eternally to live.

86.

In His Almighty hand He took the bread,
    And pour'd his plenall Blessing upon it,
Never on any but His own dear head
    Such potent Benediction did sit;
        Indeed, it was that Blessing's echo, and
        Bounded upon His Body in His hand.*

* [See the extract from Augustine, supra, pp. 15, 17. St. Cyril makes use of a corresponding phrase: "By the favor of God we approach the participation of the Mystical Eucharist, receiving Christ in our hands."—In *Johan.* xii.]

89.

Beaumont. Sweet Jesu! O how can Thy world forget
　　Their royal Saviour, and His bounty, Who
Upon their table His Ownself hath set,
　　Who in their holy cups fails not to flow
　　　　And on their dishes lie. Did ever friend
　　　　So true a token of his love commend?

90.

Infallibly there dost Thou flow, and lie.
　　Though mortal eyes discover no such thing,
Quick-sighted Faith reads all the mystery,
　　And humble, pious souls know how to bring
　　　　Into the wonder's Cabinet, and there
　　　　Make all the Jewels of this Truth appear.

91.

She generously dares on God relie,
　　And trust His word how strange so e'er it be;
If Jesus once pronounces This is my
　　Body and Blood; far, far be it, cries she,
　　　　That I should think my dying Lord would cheat
　　　　Me in His legacie of drink and meat.

92.

His word's omnipotent: by *saying*, He
　　Effects what e'er He says, and more than I
Or can or would conceive. What is't to me
　　If He transcends man's slow capacitie?
　　　　Surely it well becomes Him so to doe,
　　　　Nor were He God if He could not doe so.

93.

Let Him say what He will, I must denie
　　Him to be God, or certain hold His word:
Me it concerneth not, to verifie
　　What He proclaims: my duty's to afford
　　　　Meek credit, and let him alone to make
　　　　Good whatsoever He is pleas'd to speak.

95.   Beaumont.

Grosse and unworthy spirits sure they be
  Who of their Lord such mean conceptions frame,
That parting from His dearest consorts, He
  No token of His love bequeathed to them
      But simple bread and wine; a likely thing,
      And well becoming Heaven's magnificent King!

96.

A likely thing that when the lusty blood
  Of bulls and goats can wash no sins away,
The blood of grapes should with a stronger flood
  Quite overwhelm and drown the world's decay!
      O no, such virtue in no Blood can dwell,
      But that which through the veins of God did thrill.

97.

Ask me not then, How can the thing be done,
  What power of sense or reason can digest it?
Fools, as you are, what demonstration
  So evident as this,—my God profest it?
      And if you once can prove that He can lie,
      This wonder, and Him too, I will denie.

100.

But what thank were't if you could credit what
  To sense and reason's eye were written plain?
Heav'n's much to them beholden, who will not
  Believe it higher is than they can strain,
      Who jealous are of God, and will not be
      Induced to trust Him farther than they see.

101.

But yet had you these modest eyes of mine,
  You in this gloomie cloud would see the sun,
That sun, who wisely doth disdain to shine
  On those who, with bold prying, peep upon
      His sacred majestie, which plainly I,
      Because I make no anxious search, descrie.

104.

Beaumont. Needs will they peep into the manner how
   This hidden miracle to pass was brought,
And madly, being not content to know
   What Christ thought fit to teach them, study out
      They know not what, and *make this banquet prove*
      A Sacrament of war, and not of love.

105.

Some press too near, and spy what is not there,
   Some carelessly take what is there away,
Some will confess no miracle, for fear
   That consequent be ushered in, which they
      Resolve to stop, or that their faith should be,
      Forced to confess more than their eyes can see.

107.

Some sift existence, substance, accidents,
   Concomitance, through logick's busy sieve:
Trans, sub, and *con,* by strange experiments
   They boult so long, that they themselves deceive:
      For whilst to win the precious flour they strain,
      The coarse and refuse bran is all they gain.

108.

When Aristotle's laws are urged to be
   The umpires in religion, the rent
Poor Art would fain sew up in piety,
   Is mended but by further detriment:
      For by the unworthy clownish needle, it
      Both multiplied, and wider ope is set.

109.

O happy world, if all would once agree
   In that which Jesus did so plainly teach,
If those short words no more might tentered be
   By long disputes beyond themselves to reach:
      If they, to apprehend their sense, would strain
      Their faithful heart, and not their doubtful brain.

110.

If they their notions and themselves would cease
  To rack and torture; and to make their great
And burly volumes swell with witnesses
  Of their profound and learned want of wit:
      If for the manner they would trust their Lord,
      And for the substance take him at his word.

111.

For Heaven its faithful wheel shall sooner turn,
  And backward hale the sun into the east;
The polar bear in Lybia's furnace burn,
  And Sirius' mouth be sealed up with frost;
      Into the lofty spheres dull Tellus leap,
      And headlong tumble Height into the deep,

112.

Than any syllable which droppeth from
  The lips of Jesus can be borne away
Upon the winds' swift wings, and never come
  Back with its full effect: however they,
      Whom wit befools, will be so mad in this
      Clear point, as to dispute away their bliss.

119.

Mechanick zeale inspir'd by sottishnesse
  And by enthusiastic ordination
Of self-deluded Fancie call'd to dresse
  God's Feast in man's reformed misshapen fashion,
      Will purest purity itself defile,
      And by Heav'ns gate find out a way to Hell.

138.

By order of the prudent law of Heaven,
  No creature's blood the lip of man should stain:
And just and useful was the caution given,
  That pious mouthes might be reservéd clean,
      In reverence to the Blood of this pure Lamb,
      Designed into believing lips to stream.

139.

Beanmont

O blessed, bloody, peacefull wine! O how
  Divinely hast thou satisfaction made
For those enflaming poisons which sweet flow
  In other wines! May Noah now be glad
    Of his invention since his foule mishap
    Is clean wash'd out by this all purging grape.

140.

This wine is that wherein dwells veritie,
  The veritie of heaven; for heaven in it
All melted is: those noble joys which we
  Bathed in at home, are here together met,
    In strange epitomie, and smiling swim
    About the chalice's soul-charming brim.

151.

Oft have I seen brave spirits when they rose
  From this great Banquet, filled with generous rage,
Flie in the face of vice, and nobly choose
  Against its stoutest ramparts to engage
    Their heavenly confidence, nor has their high
    Adventure failed to reach down victory.

152.

Oft have I seen them smile in sweet disdain
  Upon misfortune's most insulting look:
Oft have I seen them kindly entertain
  Those guests faint human nature worst can brook,
    Grief, sickness, loss, oppression, calumny,
    Shame, plunder, banishment, and poverty.

153.

Oft have I seen them scorn the frown of death,
  On crosses laugh, most sweetly hug the bitter
Salute of swords, and spend their finall breath
  In wooing greatest tortures to be greater;
    Oft have I seen them enter single fight
    Both with the Peers and with the Prince of Night.

154.

For knowing well what strength they bear within,
  By stiff tenacious faith they hold it fast;
How can these champions ever fail to win,
  Who cap-a-pie, for arms, with Heaven are dressed?
      Those breasts must needs all batteries defy,
      Where God himself in garrison doth lie.

155.

But to augment the wonder, Psyche, this
  Great feast of feasts can never all be spent:
When millions are filled, entirely 't is
  The same it was, and knows no detriment;
      So, though the world all drinketh air, yet still
      The undiminished region it doth fill.

156.

And yet not so: for here each soul doth eate
  The totall banquet, and yet leaves it whole:
These antecedent ages cannot cheat
  Those which lag on behind; whilst heaven doth roll,
      And earth stand still, this ever-teeming board
      The same delights will unto all afford.

158.

Though all heaven's starry tapers lighted be
  At Phœbus' eyes, his raies keep still entire,
His image shines on every lake and sea,
  Yet only one is his original fire,
      Which doth its wondrous single self so wide
      In its compleat similitude divide.

159.

Thus, but more really than thus, this Feast
  Most absolutely one, is wholly spread
Into the mouth and heart of every guest,
  And fails not there more heavenly beams to shed
      Than when the sun, by his meridian ray
      Triumphs upon the highest throne of day.

160.

Beaumont. Thy most profoundly gracious Lord, who far
　　Above the reach of any want did reign,
Descended from his mighty glories sphere;
　　And that his voyage might be sure to gain
　　　　Him Emptiness [for] fullness, lowly He
　　　　To prove the poorer, would a borrower be.

161.

For hither on this strange adventure come,
　　He borrowed of the world humanity,
And in the cabinet of Mary's womb
　　Dressed up Himself compleatly man: yet He
　　　　Though by this condescent, new raies He set
　　　　In Nature's crown, still thought Himself in debt.

162.

Right generous as He was, He meant to pay
　　All back again which He had borrowed here,
His Body and His Blood He meant to lay
　　Upon the Crosse, and make requital there
　　　　To all his creditors, and freely by
　　　　That payment, ransome them from misery.

163.

And yet because His human nature He
　　So dearly loves, that He concludes to bear
It home in triumph, and eternally
　　Those narrow robes of bondless mercie wear:
　　　　E'er He his journey took, He plotted how
　　　　It might ascend and yet remaine below.

164.

Remaine below; and be as oft restored
　　As man would please to take it, and the way
He instituted was by this adored
　　Mysterious Banquet, which doth day by day
　　　　Repay His Flesh and Blood, that man may eat
　　　　And drink, and with his God incorporate.

165.

For, to compleat His most excessive love
  Beyond the reach of any parallel;
This noble pay He doth so far improve
  That His eternal Godhead joyns to swell
    The Royal Feast; for this can never be
    Disseveréd from His humanity.

173.

Here legions of the heavenly army keep
  The guard of reverence; round the mercy-seat
Not two, but thousand gallant cherubs peep
  With ravishment on what you drink and eat;
    Here stately principalities attend,
    Here thrones bow down, and here dominions bend.

174.

Pure is their sight, and sprightfully can passe
  Quite through that veil which on this banquet lies
A veil which in profound compassion was
  Thrown on the countenance of these mysteries,
    Which dart more glories from their naked face
    Than ever did great Moses' temples grace.

178.

When bats may venture to the eagle's nest,
  And their faint eyes against fair Titan's set;
When purblind owls may leave their gloomy roost,
  And with safe looks the face of high noon meet;
    When midnight dares throw off her sable cloak,
    And into bright Aurora's wardrobe look;

179.

Then may dim-sighted men securely gaze
  Upon their Lord's unveiléd brightness; then
May they directly to His royal face
  Without a perspective's assistance run;
    Then may they boldly scorn their eyes to shroud
    Under the shadowing courtesy of a cloud.

180.

Beaumont. But Jesus, who full well their weakness knew,
 Would in the shelter of plain wine and bread
Accommodate His goodness to their view,
 That in familiar Elements they might read
  The hidden mystery, and happier be
  Than their dust-dampéd mortal eyes could see.

183.

Alas, when time shall old and doting grow,
 And Christian spirits sympathise with it;
Man will be bold to make this banquet know
 That by its outside they will square and fit
  Their wary faith, which further must not venture
  Than blunt and feeble sense's edge can enter.

184.

Rank superstition 'tis presumed if they
 Should think God's Table holier than their own;
If to this Chalice more respect they pay
 Than to those cups which all the jolly town
  Toss in the public inns, whene'er they keep
  Their free communion of good fellowship.

185.

If they but bow the head, or bend the knee,
 Or let their humbled bodies comment on
Their lowly minds, if they but dare to be
 Professors of good manners, if they shun
  But that which love and gratitude abhors,
  They must be voted flat idolators.

190.

But those brave lovers, of whose generous breast
 Jesus entire possession holds, are so
Inamored of this soul-attracting Feast,
 That they with all the art of reverence to
  Its Board approach, and make their meek desire
  After angelick compliments aspire.

191.
Beaumont.

Their hearts beat high with that mysterious zeal
  Which fires our breasts, and fain would stoop as low
As seraphs do, whene'er this miracle
  Of love invites their reverent knees to bow:
      Fain would their panting passionate piety
      Be infinite, as is this mystery.

205.

O how her soul into the Patin leaped,
  And dived into the bottom of the Cup!
With what inamorations she weeped!
  What sighs of joy did break her bosom ope!
      How struggled fear with love, how did she groan
      Between humility and ambition.

208.

Whilst in this dainty agony she lay,
  Into her mouth the priest her wishes brings,
Which to her heart directly took their way,
  And then poured out ten thousand ravishing things,
      By which strange deluge her dear hopes were driven
      Into Creation's gulph, and drowned in heaven.

211.

Time was when Heaven in this late happy isle
  Kept open house; when this celestial feast
Did freely wooe all hearts to come and fill
  Their appetite's ambition with the best
      Of antedated bliss, and grow divine
      By this most spiritual bread and wine.

218.

O how come Christian souls so well content
  To want the choicest viands heaven could give,
O how preposterously abstinent
  Are they who with all riotous clamour strive
      To fortify the belly, but can find
      No time to victual and recruit the mind.

219.

Beaumont. More provident those heroes surely were
    Upon whose nearer hearts the warmer blood
Of Jesus dropped: not once a month, or year,
    They their devotion cheered with angels' food.
      But duly every morn His Table spread,
      And made the Lord of life their daily bread.

END OF PART I.

LONDON: G. J. PALMER, SAVOY STREET, STRAND.